International Marketing and Management Research

Series Editor
Anshu Saxena Arora, School of Business and Public Administration,
University of the District of Columbia, Washington, DC, USA

International Marketing and Management Research (IMMR) Series provides a forum for academics and professionals to share the latest developments and advances in knowledge and practice of global business and international management. The series is a uniquely positioned contribution of interrelated research papers across all business disciplines including: marketing, international business, strategy, digital strategy, organizational behavior and cross-cultural management, international marketing, international finance, global value chains, global supply chain management, sustainable innovations, e-business and e-commerce, social media, new product design and innovation, and business economics. Six volumes have been published under the IMMR series. Each research paper published in this series goes through a double-blind peer review process. Through the series, we examine the impact of cross-cultural issues, characteristics, and challenges with regard to global and sustainable business innovations; institutional and regulatory factors on international marketing and management issues; and the effects of institutional changes on global businesses with regard to both traditional and digital worlds. IMMR series fosters the exchange of ideas on a range of important international subjects, provides stimulus for research, and strengthens the development of international perspectives. The international perspective is further enhanced by the geographical spread of the contributors.

More information about this series at
https://link.springer.com/bookseries/14845

Ananya Rajagopal

Women Entrepreneurs in Emerging Markets

Managing Performance within Ecosystems

palgrave
macmillan

Ananya Rajagopal
Department of Business
and Economics
Universidad Anáhuac México
Torres de Potrero, Mexico

ISSN 2662-8546 ISSN 2662-8554 (electronic)
International Marketing and Management Research
ISBN 978-3-030-89769-7 ISBN 978-3-030-89770-3 (eBook)
https://doi.org/10.1007/978-3-030-89770-3

This Palgrave Macmillan imprint is published by the registered company Springer Nature Switzerland AG
The registered company address is: Gewerbestrasse 11, 6330 Cham, Switzerland

To my beloved son Akhilesh

Acknowledgements

Women entrepreneurship has been in the limelight of academics and social institutions since long. After attaining my doctoral specialization in entrepreneurship, I have been leaning to explore the gender perspectives in entrepreneurship. The principal insight in developing this book has emerged from the field studies of minority enterprises managed by women in Mexico such as ethnic pottery commonly known as Talavera. My research went deep into this theme, which motivated me to explore the entrepreneurial practices followed by women across developing economies including Mexico. My journey in exploring entrepreneurship across destinations in different regions has further strengthened my knowledge and insights on women enterprises. This book is an outgrowth of a long academic voyage in exploring women enterprises and finding social values associated with gender equality in economic, technological, and educational front.

I am thankful for the encouragement from Dr. Jose Balmori, Director of Business and Economics Division at Anahuac University, Mexico, to take up new research endeavors. I have been significantly educated by the comments and suggestions of various anonymous referees on my previous research works related to entrepreneurship, innovation, and marketing strategy that helped me in developing this contribution. I am eternally thankful and indebted to Dr. Rajagopal for guiding me in the writing process of this book and motivating me to always take the extra mile in all my efforts. I express my deep gratitude to Arati Rajagopal for the initial copy editing of the manuscript and for always being my guiding star. I express my sincere thanks to Marcus Ballenger, Commissioning Editor, Scholarly Business, Palgrave Macmillan, for encouraging me to work on this research and accepting the proposal for publication.

Praise for *Women Entrepreneurs in Emerging Markets*

"Entrepreneurial ecosystems are rapidly changing with the growing awareness on gender equality and empowerment of women entrepreneurs as a global agenda. This book addresses a blend of conceptual and applied discussions on women entrepreneurs with learning experience across continents... A good read for managers and researchers."

—Angappa Gunasekaran, *Director and Professor, School of Business Administration, Penn State Harrisburg, PA*

"A woman with economic empowerment is, by definition, a strong woman. However, living the empowered journey is a major challenge. The author puts forth new concepts supported by the examples on women-led enterprises across developing economies, which makes this book a worth read..."

—Jose Balmori, *Associate Dean, Business and Economics School, Universidades Anáhuac México, Mexico City*

Contents

About the Author

Ananya Rajagopal holds a Ph.D. in Administration with focus on Entrepreneurship and Marketing Strategies from EGADE Business School, Tecnológico de Monterrey. She obtained her Master of Business Administration (M.B.A.) degree from Alliant International University, San Diego, specializing in Strategic Management. She has obtained two Bachelor of Science degrees: BS Industrial and Systems Engineering from the Tecnológico de Monterrey, and BS in International Business Administration from Alliant International University, San Diego. She has ample experience in the financial industry in Mexico City since 2006.

Ananya Rajagopal has published several papers in international journals of repute and contributed research works in international conferences and edited books. Ananya Rajagopal is author of the books *Managing Startup Enterprises in Emerging Markets: Leadership Dynamics and Marketing Strategies* published in 2020 by Palgrave Macmillan; and *Epistemological Attributions to Entrepreneurial Firms: Linking Organizational Design and Operational Efficiency*, published in 2021 by Palgrave Macmillan, NY. She is reviewer of several journals of international repute including *Emerald Emerging Markets Case Studies*, *Journal of Transnational Management*, and *Journal of Strategy and Management*. She is also a member of the advisory panel of Elsevier Insights.

Ananya Rajagopal is Research Professor at Universidad Anáhuac Mexico. She has been conferred the membership of Level-I of National System of Researcher (SNI) under the aegis of National Council of Science and Technology, Government of Mexico.

List of Figures

CHAPTER 1

Introduction

Abstract Women entrepreneurs in emerging markets are gaining increasing importance in changing economic ecosystems, which are supported by the political, economic, social, technological, and legal factors. The business potential of women entrepreneurs has grown over demographic and entrepreneurial domains driven by inclusive innovation and co-creation. It has been observed that the entrepreneurial growth in emerging markets is non-linear and complex due to social stigmas and work-family imbalances. However, changing social and cultural environment play significant role in empowering women entrepreneurs and narrowing down the socio-economic constraints to perform entrepreneurial activities within and beyond niche. The family networks and social ties also play significant role in developing women entrepreneurship and connecting to upstream markets to explore potential opportunities. The preface for the book titled 'Women Entrepreneurs in Emerging Markets: Managing Performance within Ecosystems' discusses core arguments by reviewing contemporary literature and identifying embedded gaps to provide new directions towards managing women-led enterprises.

Keywords Women entrepreneurs · Emerging markets · Innovation · Co-creation · Performance management · Family networks

A. Rajagopal, *Women Entrepreneurs in Emerging Markets*, International Marketing and Management Research,
https://doi.org/10.1007/978-3-030-89770-3_1

Gender studies in entrepreneurship have been the center of academic and managerial attraction since the mid-twentieth century. The social empowerment of women has significantly contributed to the regional economic growth and social development. Consequently, social and women entrepreneurships[1] have become the critical players in under-explored entrepreneurial ecosystems and economic mainstay in the developing world. The social and economic potential spanning over demographic and entrepreneurial domains in the society have been identified as bottom of the pyramid[2] of the development perspectives. This philosophy has gained growing importance in the social entrepreneurship and inclusive innovation driven by women entrepreneurs who pioneered small-scale innovations within domestic economic field. Women entrepreneurs, who enable deprived populations not only to participate as potential customers, but also to serve as cocreators, suppliers, and producers, have emerged in the developing economies as frugal innovators for utilitarian products. Therefore, women entrepreneurs are considered as the key source of innovation and business growth. These entrepreneurs are active social agents, who gather weight in crowdsourced innovations, social capital formation, and in deriving business models from social networks.[3]

Core Arguments

The journey of women entrepreneurs moves through four stages of entrepreneurial process comprising motivation (self, family, and peers), exploring opportunity (crowdsourcing and social recognition), acquiring resources (gender promotion programs and limited own capital), and market orientation. These stages are the influential factors combined with cocreation of workplace, family environment, and gender concerns of the society. Women entrepreneurs largely function within the social and

[1] Muntean, S. C., & Ozkazanc-Pan, B. (2016). Feminist perspectives on social entrepreneurship: Critique and new directions. *International Journal of Gender Entrepreneurship, 8*(3), 221–241.

[2] Brugmann, J., & Prahalad, C. K. (2007). Cocreating business's new social compact. *Harvard Business Review, 85*(2), 80–90.

[3] Si, S., Yu, X., Wu, A., Chen, S., Chen, S., & Su Y. (2015). Entrepreneurship and poverty reduction: A case study of Yiwu China. *Asia Pacific Journal of Management, 32*(1), 119–143.

cultural contexts that influence in recognizing market-oriented opportunity. However, women entrepreneurs face a wide gap between personal ambitions and self-conceived barriers toward entrepreneurship owing to the social values. During these stages, women are more prone to using personal funding, and are less influenced by the external resource environment.[4] Entrepreneurial process among women entrepreneurs in emerging markets is nonlinear and complex due to the issues associated with work-family balance. However, women entrepreneurs undertake more creative and constructive opportunities than conventional and linear entrepreneurial patterns. Such behavior has been confirmed through various studies explaining effectuation theory, which focuses on social ventures built within subsistence economy.[5]

Social environment and cultural context play significant roles in exploring and recognizing opportunities among women entrepreneurs. However, self-perception and personal ambitions often raise self-conceived barriers toward entrepreneurial performance within social environment. The social status of women in various sociocultural environments affects entrepreneurial motivations and acquiring adequate resources to manage enterprises at the initial stage, and scaling of business in the latter.[6] The social and economic constraints experienced by women entrepreneurs affect their innovation, entrepreneurial, and marketing skills. Entrepreneurial education in women is lower than men, which causes relatively lower self-esteem, lower social status, and lower cultural sensitivity affecting the empowerment of women in entrepreneurship activities in developing economies.[7] In addition, family networks and social ties play significant role in nurturing women entrepreneurship in emerging markets, as these factors facilitate access to capital, infrastructure, human resources, and connectivity to markets. Some studies

[4] Sullivan, D. M., & Meek W. R. (2012). Gender and entrepreneurship: A review and process model. *Journal of Managerial Psychology, 27*(5), 428–458.

[5] Nahi, T. (2016). Cocreation at the base of the pyramid: Reviewing and organizing the diverse conceptualizations. *Organizational Environment, 29*(4), 416–437.

[6] Katre, A. (2018). Facilitating affective experiences to stimulate women's entrepreneurship in rural India. *International Journal of Gender Entrepreneurship, 10*(3), 270–288.

[7] Goyal, P., & Yadav V. (2014). To be or not to be a woman entrepreneur in a developing country? *Psychosociological Issues in Human Resource Management, 2*(2), 68–78.

have argued that women entrepreneurs contribute to socioeconomic development and uplift the quality of life at the bottom of the pyramid.

In view of the above discussion, this book includes entrepreneurial case studies of five major emerging economies (Brazil, India, Mexico, China, and Africa) to explore entrepreneurial attributes and practices among women entrepreneurs. A comparison of regional entrepreneurial ecosystems illustrates the commonalities and variations among the enterprises led by women in emerging economies. Accordingly, exploring and analyzing the impact of women entrepreneurship on various elements of ecosystem justifies the discussion in the book. The above focus illustrates the entrepreneurial practices within the changing socioeconomic trends in emerging markets.

In South Asia, the specific power relations associated with gender influence entrepreneurial opportunities which are culturally sensitive and hold a low level of economic growth. However, the support of public policies tends to empower women entrepreneurs through goal-oriented key programs on improving the quality of life.[8] Some studies have identified environmental barriers comprising sociocultural, economic, political, legal, and technological complexities among women entrepreneurs in Sub-Saharan Africa. These entrepreneurs face negative social belief, low-entrepreneurial attitudes, and oppressive behavior. Such psychosocial attributes demotivate entrepreneurial process among women entrepreneurs[9] Women entrepreneurs in India perceive that social empowerment is the key for managing the enterprises successfully. The sociocultural constraints experienced by women entrepreneurs in this big emerging market include ambidextrous recognitions and adequate family support to carry out independent innovations and commercialization of entrepreneurial activities, and serve as an ambassador for social change. The women cooperatives in India have been successful as they adapt to integrated social and economic measures to implement the entrepreneurial business model. Among many women enterprises in India, the organizations supported by the government and self-help

[8] Kantor, P. (2002). Gender, microenterprise success and cultural context: The case of South Asia. *Entrepreneurship Theory and Practice, 26*(4), 131–143.

[9] Amine, L. S., & Staub K. M. (2009). Women entrepreneurs in sub-Saharan Africa: An institutional theory analysis from a social marketing point of view. *Entrepreneurship Regional Development, 21*(2), 183–211.

groups include women cottage industry cooperatives (Lijjat brand), self-employed women's association (SEWA), and regional women handloom development associations. In addition, National Repository of Information for Women (NARI), Ministry of Women & Child Development, Government of India also supports women entrepreneurship movement in India through public policies, which not only enables access to capital infrastructure but also provides structured marketplace for innovative products emerging from these enterprises.[10] Women entrepreneurs play important role in creating social capital through cocreation and expansion of family networks in Islamic perspectives as well. Studies from Indonesia[11] and Pakistan[12] endorse the role of women entrepreneurs in stimulating social change and uplifting local economy.

Global Entrepreneurship Monitor (GEM) and World Bank have played motivating roles in local governments of Latin America and Caribbean (LAC) to evolve public policies to encourage women entrepreneurship. A study carried out by World Bank and International Finance Corporation reveals that more than 40% of businesses registered in LAC region are owned by women. However, women entrepreneurs face credit gap, managerial dominance, and social security in operating their ventures.[13] Most women enterprises operate in the areas of microcredit and nonfarm businesses in the LAC region. The public policies in this region tend to focus on improving the quality of women enterprises with focus on poverty reduction, microenterprise credit, and the social norms that prescribe the conventional entrepreneurial opportunities for women.[14] The public–private partnership and corporate social responsibility projects

[10] Kothari, T. (2017). Women entrepreneurs' path to building venture success: Lessons from India. *South Asian Journal of Business Studies, 6*(2), 118–141.

[11] Anggadwita, G., Mulyaningsih, H. D., Ramadani, V., & Arwiyah M. Y. (2015). Women entrepreneurship in Islamic perspective: A driver for social change. *International Journal of Business Globalisation, 15*(3), 389–404.

[12] Lindvert, M., Patel, P. C., & Wincent J. (2017). Struggling with social capital: Pakistani women micro entrepreneurs' challenges in acquiring resources. *Entrepreneurship Regional Development, 29*(7–8), 759–790.

[13] De Vita, L., Mari, M., & Poggesi, S. (2014). Women entrepreneurs in and from developing countries: Evidences from the literature. *European Management Journal, 32*(3), 451–460.

[14] Fletschner, D., & Carter, M. (2008). Constructing and reconstructing gender: Reference group effects and women's demand for entrepreneurial capital. *The Journal of Socio-Economics, 37*, 672–693.

implemented by multinational companies like Nestlé (organic coffee farming, Colombia), Starbucks (coffee farming extension program, Mexico), and Cactus Power Mexico (Economic Empowerment for Rural Girls and Women, Mexico) are also helping women entrepreneurs to focus on cocreated business models and restructure organizational design to scale-up their business.[15] However, various limitations have been identified in many Mexican enterprises on entrepreneurial knowledge, skills, and decision-making in the context of changing market trends and technology. Women enterprises in Mexico lack in three prominent dimensions, which include design-to-market (branding and communication), organizational design (human capital and skills management), and technology acceptance (commercializing innovations and developing crowd-based business models). Consequently, women enterprises in Mexico face complexities in achieving competitive performance and market leadership[16]

Women entrepreneurs in emerging economies are guided by public policies toward developing new perceptions, understanding entrepreneurial ecosystem, and consumer behavior. These entrepreneurs widely promote their businesses based on chronological experiences and through critical examination of lessons drawn on longitudinal entrepreneurial behavior. These enterprises commonly evolve from family business foundations (FBF) and are confined to niche. They tend to explore and expand their business by seeking new opportunities across the industries and seek public policy support on capital formation to adapt to new innovations and technological trends. However, FBFs owned by women entrepreneurs lack the consistent knowledge base to run their enterprises independently. Most women-led enterprises operate partially within the triadic knowledge base: acquired knowledge, interrelated knowledge, and self-perceived knowledge base. They lack in critically examining the business philosophies and gaining benefit from the entrepreneurial perspectives to develop sustainable strategies. These enterprises initiate low-profile business in their early stages of growth

[15] Lagarda, A. M., Madrigal, D. F., & Flores, M. T. (2016). Factors associated with learning management in Mexican micro-entrepreneurs. *Estudios Gerenciales, 32*(141), 381–386.

[16] Maldonado, G., & Martinez, M. (2012). Gestión del conocimiento y crecimiento en la Pyme manufacturera de Aguascalientes (México). *Cuadernos de Administración, 28*(47), 25–36.

producing confined values to primary stakeholders, beneficiaries, and customers. However, scaling of business among women entrepreneurs has always been a major socioeconomic challenge.[17]

Review of Contemporary Literature and Gaps

In view of the changing dynamics of local–global entrepreneurship, the role of women entrepreneurs significantly affects the schematic growth of entrepreneurial market. Such phenomenon calls for extensive thinking across spatial and temporal dimensions to restructure the organizational development, change in business practices, and manage disruptions in local enterprises led by women. The existing literature on women entrepreneurship in emerging markets categorically focuses on specific attributes like resource management, innovation, and marketability of entrepreneurial products. Nonetheless, there is paucity of management resources, which exhibit integrated perspectives of women entrepreneurs considering the longitudinal (over time) and latitudinal (across geo-demographic segments). The women entrepreneurs lack in experimentation, entrepreneurial commitment, agility, and strategic alliances to reduce entrepreneurial uncertainties.[18] This book serves as a consolidated think-tank on interrelated entrepreneurial perspectives at the grassroots, with focus on change management, public policies, corporate social responsibility, organized marketplace, and sustainability in entrepreneurship.

Frugal innovation (business modeling) and reverse accountability (organizational design) are based on the theory of competitive entrepreneurship, which has not been discussed much in the existing literature. It is unclear how emerging enterprises led by women transform their business model through changing entrepreneurial perspectives and

[17] Lingelbach, D., Sriram, V., Mersha, T., & Saffu, K. (2015). The innovation process in emerging economies: An effectuation perspective. *Entrepreneurship Innovation, 16*(1), 5–17.

[18] Chandler, G. N., DeTienne, D. R., McKelvie, A., & Mumford T. V. (2011). Causation and effectuation processes: A validation study. *Journal of Business Venturing, 26*(3), 375–390.

dynamic capabilities.[19] Upon critically examining the theory of disruption and the theory of competitive entrepreneurship, the book illustrates the role of women entrepreneurs and their socioeconomic contributions over the classical entrepreneurial values. As stated earlier, most women enterprises at the bottom of the pyramid evolve from family business models within the socioeconomic environment. It is necessary to critically examine the motivations for entrepreneurship in relation to the social cognitive theory[20] Guided by this theory, the book addresses entrepreneurial and business factors that influence women-led enterprises within their social and economic environments. Accordingly, business perspectives for women entrepreneurs are based on cognitive beliefs, intrinsic and extrinsic needs, demographic factors; and ability to adapt to innovation and technology trends, explore new resources (capital and human resources), and develop sustainable organizational design which are discussed in this book. In addition, the business model theory for women entrepreneurs has been integrated with hybrid perspectives (3D paradigm: digitization, disruption, and diversification in the core discussions of the book, which categorically bridges the gap in the existing literature in terms of conventional entrepreneurship practices and applied business modeling in carrying out entrepreneurial activities within sociocultural domain. The book has evolved around the discussions on gender-based social maxims and their role in restructuring operational and organizational designs of women-led enterprises. In addition, the book aims at measuring the performance of these enterprises in the context of inter- and intra-organizational alliances to improve entrepreneurial performance. It also discusses effectiveness of marketing strategies, causes and effects of marketing strategies on entrepreneurial performance, organizational design practices, and design-to-market concept in the context of contemporary organizational and operational designs. Schematic discussion of the book is exhibited in Fig. 1.1.

The book discusses core and prereferral topics relationally and relevantly in each chapter to keep the promise of the book. The broad topic

[19] Dong, J. Q. (2019). Moving a mountain with a teaspoon: Toward a theory of digital entrepreneurship in the regulatory environment. *Technological Forecasting and Social Change, 146*, 923–930.

[20] Wang, S., Hung, K., & Huang, J. W. (2019), Motivations for entrepreneurship in the tourism and hospitality sector: A social cognitive theory perspective, *International Journal of Hospitality Management, 78*, 78–88.

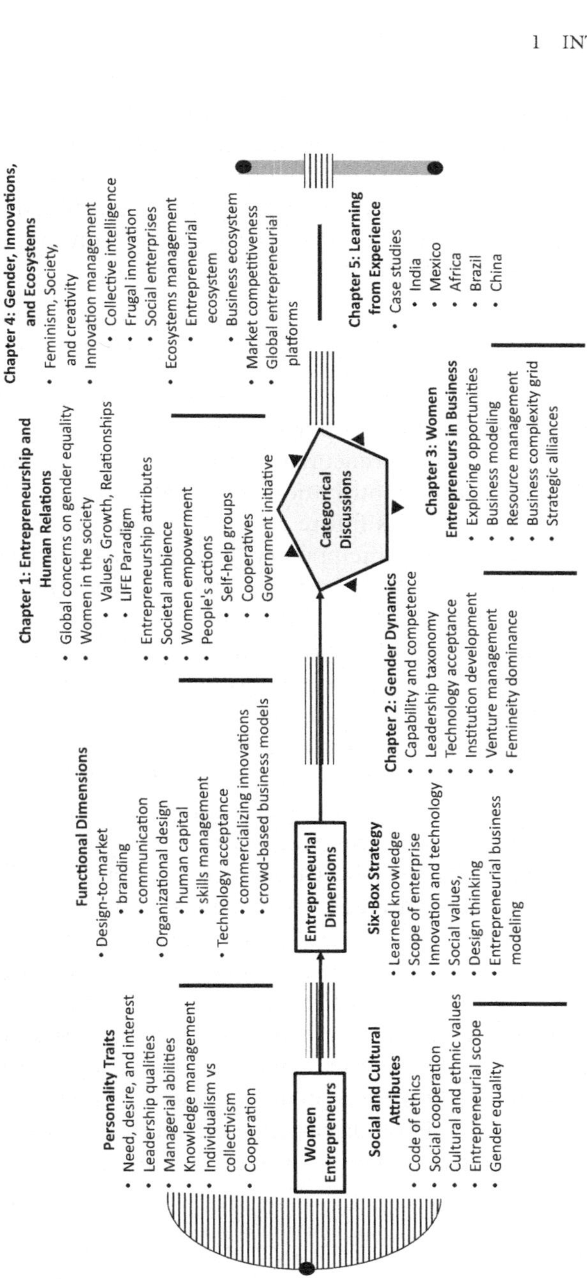

Fig. 1.1 Schematic discussion paradigm (*Source* Author)

of the book is to discuss the socioeconomic attributes of the women entrepreneurs in emerging markets, supplementing them with the case studies purposively selected in the four rapidly emerging economies. This justifies the scope of the book and discussion map as illustrated in the above Fig. 1.1. The focus of the book is largely on convergence of entrepreneurial attributes and practice.

Thematic Significance and Core Contributions

This book provides a balanced view of entrepreneurial dynamics within gender-based social frameworks, and portrays the organizational design, operational efficiency, and entrepreneurial governance at the bottom of the industry. Therefore, this contribution adds value to the existing literature. It proactively motivates future research on organizational and operational design based on contemporary best practices, managerial reviews, public policy performances, and theoretical attributions. It also contributes toward strategic management of women-led enterprises in context of the changing leadership taxonomy, employee engagement, and stakeholder accountability to achieve market competitiveness and organizational growth.[21]

The rapidly changing enterprise-management system provides agility in organizational design, operational efficiency, and strategy development. The increasing opportunities of organizational design and shifts in the operational patterns have triggered chaos in the market, which needs to be meticulously handled by women-led enterprises within the span of their resources. The strategic implications of PESTEL factors (Political, economic, social, technological, environmental, and legal) on management of these enterprises are discussed in this book. The strategic decisions on improving organizational efficiencies comprising employee engagement, stakeholder value management, collective leadership, participatory organizational design, and team management add applied value to the book. This book is based on conceptual discussions related to women entrepreneurship, and disseminates knowledge on applied perspective on women entrepreneurship through the existing case studies in emerging

[21] *e.g.* Henninger, P., Brem, A., Giones, F., Bican, P. M., & Wimschneider, C. (2020). Effectuation vs. causation: Can established firms use start-up decision-making principles to stay innovative? *International Journal of Innovation Management, 24*(01), https://doi.org/10.1142/S1363919620500024

markets. The book has a blend of conceptual and applied entrepreneurial perspectives in lieu of the primary database research.

This book focuses on social perspectives of women entrepreneurship, which has been discussed in the work context of work-life balance, crowd-based business modeling (as most women entrepreneurs collect business ideas through crowdsourcing), and economic perspectives associated with quality-of-life expectations. The core focus of this book is toward converging business perspectives with social values and lifestyle. The above elements of discussion distinguish this book from the previous literature, which is widely focused on leadership, gender, and family entrepreneurship. This book discusses attributes of women entrepreneurship in developing economies with focus on new entrepreneurial trends, changing organizational design and workplace environment, frugal innovation, and technology, and shifts in market behavior. The book integrates six-box strategy including learned knowledge, scope of enterprise, innovation and technology, social values, design-development, and entrepreneurial business modeling. The core debate in this book is about critically examining the entrepreneurial evidence toward establishing practical, tacit, and intuited strategies to redesign entrepreneurial business models and reinforce positive social values for women entrepreneurs. It bridges the strategic gaps to improve entrepreneurial efficacy through six-box strategy paradigm and explains how competitive business models help in improving the applied dimensions of entrepreneurship at the bottom of the pyramid.[22] This book analyzes positivist, constructivist, pragmatist, interpretivist, and phenomenological perspectives to explain entrepreneurial behavior of women and derive cognitive synthesis to enhance business performance, entrepreneurial mindset, and perceptual schema.

This book presents a panoramic view of attributes of women entrepreneurs and practices embedded in women-led enterprises. There is a marginal discussion on entrepreneurial theories, as the core focus of the book is to present a managerial outlook of enterprises managed by women at the niche segment in emerging markets. The core theme of the book revolves around women entrepreneurship and supplements the applied perspectives across the regions with the broad framework of

[22] Berglund, H., Dimov, D., & Wennberg, K. J. (2018). Beyond bridging rigor and relevance: The three-body problem in entrepreneurship. *Journal of Business Venturing Insights, 9*(1), 87–91.

entrepreneurial ecosystem. Therefore, the discussions in all chapters are streamlined and symbiotically cohesive with salient attributes of women entrepreneurship. Also, the structure of the book has been systematically designed to discuss systemic outlook on women entrepreneurship in emerging markets.

My previous research published in various refereed academic outlets on entrepreneurship, epistemological reviews, frugal innovation, and marketing in the context of developing economies have provided the foundation of this book. The conceptual paradigms presented in this book have also been benefitted by my previous research and enriched the contents and thematic discussions. The principal audience of this book are potential researchers interested in carrying out research based on entrepreneurial practices and their contributions to organizational design and operational efficiency in women-led enterprises.

This book proposes future research directions on women entrepreneurship and business models contextual to the developing economies. This book also serves as a reference for the students of graduate management programs studying in entrepreneurship stream for learning the gender-based entrepreneurial management patterns in emerging markets. I hope that this book will be a welcome addition to the existing literature on women entrepreneurship in developing economies.

October 30, 2021 Ananya Rajagopal
Mexico City, Mexico

CHAPTER 2

Entrepreneurship and Human Relations

Abstract This chapter discusses perspectives on gender equality that have grown international in the context of equal opportunities in entrepreneurship among men and women. The social discrepancies in the human values in general and among women in particular have been discussed in this chapter in the context of changing values, economic growth, human relationships, and LIFE philosophy of women entrepreneurs. The LIFE framework has been explained with the attributes of liberty, intelligence, fraternity, and equity among women entrepreneurs. The empowerment of women has been argued in this chapter in the context of people's action and public policies.

Keywords Gender equity · Women and society · LIFE paradigm · Relationship and work-life balance · Women entrepreneurs · Empowerment

The society has undergone drastic changes in the past six decades for bridging the gap between the need for women empowerment and unequal economic opportunities. This gap still appears to be a far cry, though much tripartite efforts from the government, corporate, and social end have been invested in generating consciousness, applauding the role of women in the society, highlighting the economic inequality, and

A. Rajagopal, *Women Entrepreneurs in Emerging Markets*, International Marketing and Management Research,
https://doi.org/10.1007/978-3-030-89770-3_2

comparing the discrepancies in the work-life balance among both genders. However, it is difficult to identify how much success has been accrued in empowering women and equalizing their stakes in economic activities. The segregation of women's contribution in the society has led to subservient behavior toward the inequal treatment, emotional exploitation, verbal abuse, and workplace discrimination. The gender-based biasness is deep rooted in the society in developing economies, which portrays the implicit and explicit behavioral traits built on preconceived values embedded since childhood. It is difficult to change such outlook rapidly as people tend to develop congruence with the real-life examples, which are often hard to refute (Women in the workplace, 2020). Nonetheless, the prevalence of such outlook sets aside the entrepreneurial skills, attitudinal traits, strategic outlook, and entrepreneurial competence, and focuses on the gender of the entrepreneur to determine the rate of success or failure. Such myopic perspective along with gender-based biasness tend to hinder the socioeconomic and business growth of women entrepreneurs in emerging markets.

The analysis of economic, political, and sociocultural inequalities, therefore, is crucial in identifying the reasons causing limited economic opportunities, decision-making abilities, and strategic choices. These factors largely remain unattended and have shown significant spill-over effect on the social structure. The role of gender in entrepreneurship is based on psychosocial perceptions within the society in emerging markets. Entrepreneurial traits, competencies, and business influence the perception of investors, consumers, and the market which, in turn, affect the entrepreneurial potential and success (Ward et al., 2019). Reconstitution of business ambiance and society with focus on gender equity remains very slow. The concern of family, society, business partners, and decision-makers causes stress and burnout among women entrepreneurs, which transpires through their mindset, thus limiting the extent of economic contribution. Inadequate support from public policies and sociocultural pillars pushes women entrepreneurs to accept unrealistic working conditions to succeed in the challenging marketplace. Due to these barriers, a significant number of working women or entrepreneurs are forced to leave the workforce or downgrade their professional careers. It seems that there is a marginal shift in the long-standing social discrepancies toward women in emerging economies. However, the rate of this shift is minimal as feminist movements have attempted to produce cultural awareness and workplace equity to uplift the participation of women in business ambiance. It has been observed that the influx of institutional and private capital in entrepreneurial ventures plays a catalytic role in building cross-cultural workplace ambience, which helps in reducing social bias toward participation of woman in generating income and contributing economically to the family and society.

The United Nations has included a goal toward attaining gender equality and women empowerment within Sustainable Development Goals. The issues related to gender equality still remain critical not only in developing economies, but also in developed countries. Social organizations continuously make efforts to drive changes in society, culture, and the perception of people toward gender equality. Such drive may lead to exponential benefits with support from government initiatives. Public policies in emerging markets can play an important role in fast-tracking the process of bridging the gap in gender equity through gradual social change initiatives, active public–private initiatives, empowering nongovernmental organizations, and improving legal and fiscal measures. The positive changes toward gender equity and equality have been observed in some of the developed countries. For example, in Singapore, the participation of women in workplace doubled in 46 years, of which major increase in this was seen in the twenty-first century due to implementation of various employee-oriented corporate strategies (work-life balance, maternity benefits, childcare benefits, etc.) and public policies (subsidies, tax relief packages for working mothers, institutional support for childcare, etc.). Similarly, Japan offers 30 weeks paternity to generate consciousness about equity in parenting activities concerning a newborn child (Gupta et al., 2019). Such public policies draw the attention of the society toward the unmeasured, unpaid, or underpaid contribution of women at home and at workplace, which leads to a change of mindset toward the role of women.

Gender inequality not only poses the risk of discrimination in society, but also causes high costs to private institutions and public enterprises. Therefore, it is necessary for the public policies to aim at enhancing entrepreneurial training, promoting legal rights, easy accessibility of services, and availability of subsidized financial services in addition to redesigning vocational education curriculums to boost gender participation. These actions not only improve the position of women in the social, economic, and political arenas, but also increase productivity at the workplace, which acts as a shift in the outlook toward rebuilding equity among men and women (Charlesworth & Banaji, 2019). Policy makers and business leaders need to empower women and consider them as equal partners in the society and in the business environment to establish equitable environment in developing economies. A coalition between policy makers and business leaders will strengthen the role of women and facilitate the implementation of gender-neutral laws, social practices, and cultural change. Based on the study by Field and Tsvetkov (2020), the biasness against a particular gender is founded on low self-esteem because of prevailing male dominance in the society, tendency to criticize actions different from one's values, and lack of trust in the gender-related capabilities. The results of the study indicate that social biases give rise to the attitude of passing unsubstantiated judgements demeriting the capacities and capabilities. Consequently, social biases lead to an increase in the subjective domains within the society. Such attitude affects the women entrepreneurs and employees adversely, as it is difficult to identify and mitigate its effect on the gender discrimination.

According to Auerswald and Dani (2017), economic and entrepreneurial ecosystems are designed to maintain the equilibrium among different variables that interact within the boundaries of society and marketplace. The economic gains within the ecosystem distribute the risk across entrepreneurs, stakeholders, and market players. The entrepreneurial success bridges the gaps between financial and social disparities in developing countries. Encouraging the economic empowerment facilitates womens' participation in having a financial independence and contributing to the economy of the household. Such empowerment also allows women to have a voice and control in the decisions of business as well as household. The economic ecosystem provides women a platform for sharing economic and social benefits with their stakeholders, consumers, and family and helping in maintaining work-life balance.

Gender Equity Prism

Gender equity can be interpreted as the just treatment among genders in compliance with their needs and rights. This concept is very different from gender equality which explains that the rights, responsibilities, opportunities, and treatment are independent of the gender of a person. In many emerging economies, there has been a lack of holistic view regarding gender equality and equity to attain a sustainable development. Gender equity in general includes women's right to education, financial independence, right to decisions related to their health and body, and fair pay at workplace. These attributes of gender equity are present in the society, however, in practice they exist implicitly in the minds of the people and do not resurge in the day-to-day treatment of women, which imbalances the social and economic structure of the country. On a global scale, such imbalance leads to operational incapacity of the government bodies and public policies to drive a change in the social mindset toward empowerment of women. The gender equity prism presented in Fig. 1.1 explains the three facets (frontal, lateral, and rear) that coexist in the social and economic ecosystem.

Public policies need to implement changes from the bottom of the socioeconomic pyramid to have a sustainable impact on the empowerment initiatives for women entrepreneurs. This approach sets a potential milestone toward empowerment of women by generating awareness, engagement of women entrepreneurs, information retention, easy accessibility, and financial feasibility toward equitable business opportunities. While doing so government and nongovernment organizations (NGOs) need to develop cost effective and customized programs to educate and develop skills of women entrepreneurs, and implement them as people's collaborative project at the bottom of the socioeconomic pyramid. Nonetheless, it is important to consider the risks, challenges, and possible rewards of investing in the formation of women-entrepreneurial skills despite the pedagogical and strategic challenges. Therefore, the government and NGOs, need to recognize pedagogical challenges for implementing acquired knowledge in developing business strategies, and inculcate administrative skills and financial insight to manage the limited resources efficiently (Pearson, 2015).

Women-led enterprises face more challenges in emerging economies as compared to the developed nations due to limited resources, insufficient funding sources, operating in niche markets, inadequate infrastructure, and unstructured regulatory policies. The entrepreneurial ecosystem consisting of these challenges stimulates alternatives for improving the exiting public policies and codesigning a bottom-up entrepreneurial ecosystem (Ghosh et al., 2011).

Front Facet

The primary component of the gender equity prism explains the fundamental rights of citizens, and how these rights have been recognized for women and men within a society. In principle, fundamental rights are a set of privileges, which are recognized by the apex court and formed as a part of the constitution of a country. Gender empowerment through fundamental rights strengthens the sustainable economic development of emerging markets. Exercising the fundamental rights allows people to shape their decisions toward work, life, personal growth, social development, and financial support to overcome the prevailing discrimination, biasness, and prejudice toward various elements of the society. It is important to clarify that economic and social development is not only about changing the trivial attributes that hinder the growth, but it is also about empowering voice-of-the-people and shaping solutions to promote equity-based autonomy (Guido, 2018). Economic and social development is a tool which brings enormous change in gender issues if implemented effectively. On the contrary, it may also counteract and obstruct the fundamental rights of the people. The public policies must be implemented as a people-centered approach based on gender inclusivity, availability of resources, and time management.

Social empowerment can be explained as building autonomy, self-concept, and confidence to improve relationships across social strata. In many developing economies, large numbers of families depend on female earning members, putting women as the head of the family. This has led women to experience outside the box and lead their families irrespective of the unwelcoming discrimination of the society toward women leaders and female entrepreneurs. Such predominating practices hinder self-confidence, intrinsic motivation, and autonomy of women, hence creating a void in the society for individual and collective growth. Therefore, the social relationships need to be founded on attributes such as education, equal opportunities, belongingness, building self-identity, leadership traits, and self-confidence to build intercommunity interactions and enhance the social empowerment (Blomkvist, 2003). Social empowerment of women tends to mobilize women-led initiatives and development of female leaders in enterprises, society, and political ambiance. The process of accelerating the opportunities within the paradigm of equity, power, and dignity is enabled by the political and social opportunities and achievements, which enables women's commitment to excel in their desired prospect. Empowering women in the society is a process that includes many dimensions and helps in eliminating conventional social norms to obtain freedom, voice-of-women, and position in the male-dominated society (Bayeh, 2016).

Across history, society, economy, and politics have been mainly dominated by men, where the social dominance is represented by power and superiority to female gender. Even at present times, it is difficult to find a balanced presence of men and women in strategic positions, leadership roles, and emerging enterprises. The **3Fs** model represented by **F**amily (financial resources, trust, work-life balance), **F**raternity (social liberty, voice-of-women, community participation), and **F**undamental rights, explains the basic concepts of equity. The voice-of-women promotes the presence of women in senior-level positions, sensibilize the society toward gender perspectives, and draws attention toward respecting women's rights. However, such outlook also tags with negativity toward the treatment of women. Instead of giving them the protection from social discriminatory practices and biased gender policies, voice-of-women initiatives are transformed into a 'women as victim' approach, which negatively affects the approach to consider women as equals to men in the social, political, and cultural ambiance (Sundstorm et al., 2017). Though social awareness toward voice-of-women is high, there is an enormous gap between encouragement and effects. Predominated social stereotype culture does not allow the society to exhibit an empathetic behavior toward women. Nonetheless, women step up to leadership roles to overcome conflicts and social stereotypes toward participation of women in the economy of the household and the society, for self-motivation, and migration. Women's education is one of the perennial challenges faced by many developing countries, as the voice-of-women depends on the learning capabilities and knowledge dispersion possibilities, leading to socioeconomic development. Fundamental barriers for addressing these challenges are due to the lack of economic empowerment, poverty, education, and dependence of social proscriptions (Gholipour et al., 2010).

Empowerment of women has a positive influence on the well-being of the family, financial stability, and the psychosocial impact on the members of the family. Women empowerment also enhances self-esteem, ability to tolerate, and community upliftment to efficiently manage sustainable growth pattern. The major challenge in empowering women in developing countries is to reduce the gender gap prevalent in the social and business institutions. These institutions help in expanding their strategic outlook toward women entrepreneurs by inculcating creativity and quality in business, at the same time improving the ability to choose and perceive the value of the brands by the consumers. The institutional barriers such as family responsibilities, childcare limitations, and taxation faced by women entrepreneurs limit their involvement in business. Therefore, the government, nongovernment organizations, and public policy makers focus on encouraging the institutional influences affecting the intrinsic factors such as motivation and intention of women entrepreneurs toward offering innovative products and services in the marketplace. It is important to consider the social and cultural limitations that affect women entrepreneurs to have less diverse business network to expand their business at a rate similar to men-led entrepreneurial ventures. However, such limitations can overcome the implementation of Ambassadors' program, which highlights celebrity women entrepreneurs as role models to encourage female-led businesses, influence potential women-led entrepreneurs, and attempt to change government policies to promote entrepreneurship among women in developing nations (OCED, 2017) (Fig. 2.1).

Rear Facet

Education is an important tool for the economic growth of any country. However, developing nations find it challenging to educate their population as they face economic, social, and cultural limitations. Under such conditions, women face major challenge to outperform men and overcome the social identity as care givers and housewives despite the potential to grow economically. Consequently, public policies and nongovernment organizations have focused on educating women in informal sectors of the economy and teaching them technical skills in order to make them self-sufficient and financially independent (Guinee, 2014). The **3Es** model discusses the socioeconomic empowerment and social objectification as part of women **E**mpowerment, the values and emotions perceived by the stakeholders and consumers, using psychosocial dynamics to empower women as part of **E**ngagement, and **E**ntrepreneurial activities through economic equity and profitability of the business orientation. Empowerment of women in developing countries largely depends on the social structure, individual experiences, and circumstantial to the existing cultural norms, values, and taboos. However, being educated does not benefit the women much if they are not given equal opportunities and equity in remunerations, professional advancements, and decision-making process. Education gives independence to women, where they can make their own decisions based on logical reasoning, ability to choose between

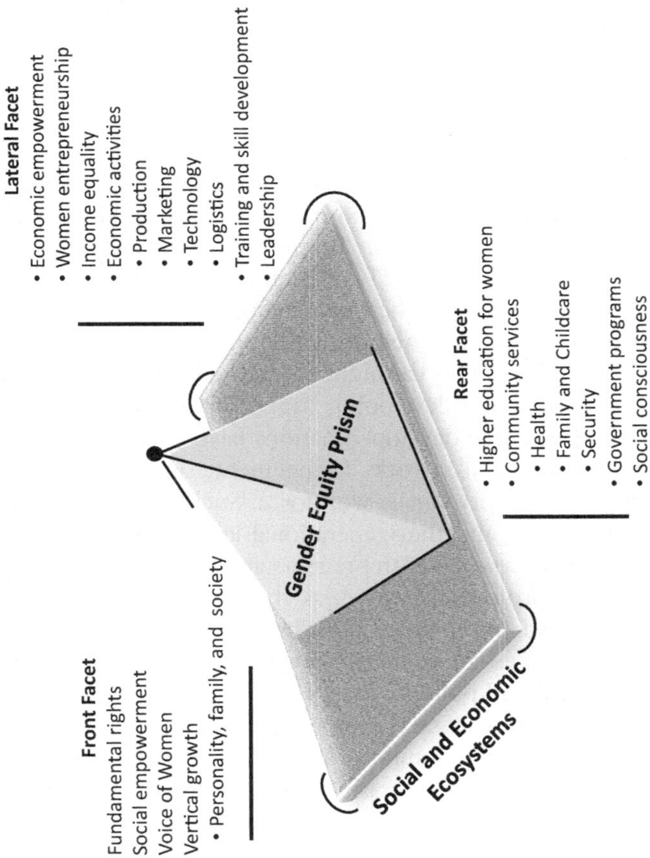

Fig. 2.1 Gender equity prism (*Source* Author)

personal and professional growth, enhance self-confidence, and disrupt predominating stereotypes (Suarez-Ortega & Galvez-Garcia, 2017).

In developing nations, family, health, and security programs have been implemented by nongovernment bodies, which aim at enhancing the participation of people in community upliftment programs. Such programs build capacity in the community to improve economic self-sufficiency and freedom among women through active participation of microenterprises, leading to an improvement in the family wellness and develop work-family balance. Most women irrespective of employment and higher gross earnings as compared to men, invest more time and energy than their spouses in unproductive household activities, which significantly diminishes the potential of success in enterprises governed by women. This, in addition to the gender expectations, childcare duties, and entrepreneurial mindset affects the health and security of the households negatively (Wang et al., 2021). Recently, women in workforce have encountered an increase in their caregiving roles and responsibilities, which has jeopardized their ability to perform efficiently and make progress in their workplace. This has highlighted the inefficient infrastructure in developed as well and developing countries toward management of childcare challenges. Some developed nations have implemented long-term paternity leaves, flexible work arrangement, and diversity—and inclusion strategies to support female workforce. Such policies encourage workplace professionalism and transgenerational leadership in improving the local economy. Also, women entrepreneurs are discouraged by people in their personal and professional circle, as they are not able to obtain equity funds to establish and improve their market offering. It is evident that the barriers for success of women entrepreneurs are huge and real, which demands a social and political change to disrupt these barriers and promote a successful and dynamic economic growth.

Individuals within a social community share certain values, knowledge, collective know-hows, and idiosyncrasies. The collective awareness and idiosyncrasies are linked to social consciousness, and it is intertwined with self-consciousness and the social-self-concept. It is difficult for people to view these attributes separately from the society. The compatibility of an individual's intrinsic moral values with the collective values of the society generates social consciousness such as family values, religious upbringing, social biases, and cultural beliefs (Parris & McInnis-Bowers, 2017). Business models based on social consciousness are influenced by the social factors, which empower women leadership in entrepreneurial firms to engage customers and stakeholders in entrepreneurial policies. Social consciousness has a profound impact on women entrepreneurs as it allows local and small entrepreneurs to collaborate with large industries. Such alliance permits local or small women-led enterprises to improve their internal policies, sales strategies, and operations management to gain sustainable growth opportunities in the marketplace. Social consciousness drives the attention of consumers toward conscious consumerism; and inclusive businesses with an objective to not only improve the product offering, but also educate consumers and market (Subramanian, 2017).

Lateral Facet

Women entrepreneurs face many obstacles in achieving economic empowerment due to lack of leadership styles within the enterprise. Women entrepreneurs also face psychological and cultural limitations apart from economic constraints due to differences in entrepreneurial mindsets. The type of mindset in men (competitiveness and profit orientation) drives their high performance in the market as compared to the female mindset (sustainable growth and long-term customer relations) which tends to slow their growth and entrepreneurial performance in the market. In this context, personal attributes and business skills play an important role in deriving success among women entrepreneurs in developing economies. However, the time invested in business by male entrepreneurs is more than the female entrepreneurs, as the latter diversify their attention toward household issues and diversion of business resources for household upliftment due to family and social pressures. Therefore, training on efficient resource management, sales force management, and effective control measures on productivity and expenditure would reduce the crowding-out effect of women enterprises (Siba, 2015). Apart from enhancing soft skills, rethinking of training on entrepreneurial perspectives needs to be developed in the context of gender identities. Managing changes in the mindsets of women entrepreneurs and consumers, and social paradigms, is a somewhat difficult proposition and should be customized by the requirements of entrepreneurs. In addition, training the women entrepreneurs not only on financial skills, but also on basic business skills, work-life balance techniques, and usage of technological advances is needed. The above determinants have demonstrated an increase in the success of women-led entrepreneurial ventures.

Women entrepreneurs in developing economies face many challenges such as societal inequality, lack of business orientation, insufficient educational provision, and impediments in securing financial support. Government programs are often criticized for ineffective implementation due to administrative process and government infrastructure. These programs should be directed toward the development and implementation of business orientation and skill development programs in congruence with the market dynamics to support women entrepreneurs. The innovative pedagogical programs can educate women and empower them to establish themselves in the marketplace by making efficient use of constrained resources. However, income inequality is a major issue that stands as a breach between the low- and high-capital enterprises. Such gap is growing at an overwhelming rate across the developing countries. Women entrepreneurs need to be guided through government and social organizations to find opportunities and acquire funds for entrepreneurial development. Such social and political advocacy would help to reduce the gap among opportunity, marketing, technology, income, and growth. Such efforts would be able to reduce the gap of income inequality between men and women in the society. Women entrepreneurs face both objective and subjective issues in their work-life balance including family responsibilities and work pressures (Pinkovetskaia et al., 2019).

Women in Society: The Convergence Path

The entrepreneurial dynamics in the society is based on rapidly changing socioeconomic drivers such as quality of life, gender identity, social development, entrepreneurial equity, and social and income equality. Women have been conformed to the societal and gender norms for their social well-being including the way they express emotions and look feminine. However, the contemporary challenge among women entrepreneurs also calls for robust behavioral attributes at par with men entrepreneurs. The ability of women to liberate from such preestablished social stereotypes and step ahead to participate in the sociopolitical and economic arenas attributes to the true concept of empowerment of women. Public policies, government programs, and cultural dynamics help in empowering women to improve their quality of life and values. Social empowerment of women mainly focuses on gender inequalities, equal opportunities, and financial freedom, while psychological empowerment is closely linked with the social empowerment, which motivates self-interests and promotes economic and social equality. Such motivations drive economic growth and promote power relations toward the entrepreneurial behavior of women in developing economies (Khan & BiBi, 2011). The attributes associated with women-entrepreneurial behavior include exploring market opportunities, innovative tenacity, planning and organization, and leadership skills. Female entrepreneurs are generally found to have a disadvantage over sociability as their personal ecosystem (work-life balance, business opportunity, and professional growth) interferes with their social ecosystem (equal business opportunities, social networks, status of women, and gender development). One of the core attributes of any entrepreneur is the lack of risk averse outlook, which appears to be limited among women entrepreneurs (Patrick et al., 2016).

The success of women entrepreneurs is not solely attributed to their business skills but also to their soft skills such as planning and organization, transformational leadership, motivation, and resource management. Women entrepreneurs tend to manage effectively the internal and external stakeholder and employee development programs to build loyalty and trust. In addition, the strategic outlook is identified as the connection between personal and social ecosystem of women entrepreneurs. The strategic outlook nurtures the ability of women entrepreneurs toward determining strategic goals, identifying and mitigating risks, aligning tactics with strategic goals, decision-making process based on cost–benefit analysis, and setting up the actions for implementation of strategic objectives (Mohammed et al., 2017). Global concern on gender development is considered as a core variable for implementing institutional change, promoting gender equity, and social growth through sustainable development. Gender development programs aim at promoting gender equality, cultural change, and social acceptance in order to draw attention toward the disadvantages, unequal power roles, expectations and stereotypes faced by working women and women entrepreneurs. Inclusive strategies promote rigorous gender analysis, which helps in identification, understanding, and effective implementation of gender development plans in the socioeconomic arenas. Gender-enhanced sustainable development embeds inclusivity, knowledge and skills, financial stability, cultural changes, and social aspects to promote positive social impact through inclusive decision-making process. Social agenda includes gender development plans on workforce balance, equal access to resources, and efficient management of resources (Abebe, 2015).

The push factors converging with the pull factors focus on the needs, problems, and challenges faced by women entrepreneurs in the society. The initiatives and solutions supported by the governments through public policies, and the process of creating value through commercialization of innovative products and services help in building triadic enterprise structure comprising the design-to-market, design-to-society, and design-to-value ecosystems (Rajagopal, 2021). As women entrepreneur face manifold challenges, need for motivation, strategic direction, and administrative control, it is necessary to provide an integrated enterprise development program to inculcate creativity and innovation in women-led enterprises to drive market competitiveness. Women entrepreneurs tend to develop and maintain long-term relationships, communicate with clarity, and act as a source of inspiration for other women, which enables them to attain a sustainable entrepreneurial growth. The problem-solving capacity of women entrepreneurs has been considered as a strong driving force in the corporate and industrial ambiance. The initiative taken up by women entrepreneurs in reference to technological advances, innovation-led products and services, and business outlook allows them to engage more talent in the workplace and tends to balance the participation of both genders in their established workplace (Connell, 2005). Such stance provides economic empowerment to women in the society and fosters inclusive and sustainable development of the stakeholders in the enterprise, making it imperative to women in developing economies. Therefore, governments, through public policies, should encourage women entrepreneurs to develop and promote innovative products and services by contributing to employment and economic growth of the country. The cultural and social values adhere women entrepreneurs from progressing in their entrepreneurial ventures. The influence of tradition and culture appears to be stronger than the influence of legal and regulatory process during the decision-making process in women-led enterprises. In some developing economies, women entrepreneurship is seen as an inappropriate choice of profession, as it goes against the traditional and religious beliefs incrusted within the society. Therefore, by promoting women's empowerment and women entrepreneurship, local populations are trained within cooperatives. For example, the shea belt in Mali known as *women's gold*, provides more than 80% of income to the local women through 156 women's cooperatives, which employ more than 1200 local women (Elias & Carney, 2007). Figure 1.2 explains the convergence path between society, entrepreneurship, and women profiles through the push and pull factors (Fig. 2.2).

The core principle in implementing the public initiatives in the society focuses on understanding the market dynamics and adapting to the changes occurring in the community. The social values promoted through the objective-driven focus contribute to an enormous impact on social change. The combination of social change with business objectives demands a specific skill set to significantly exhibit the social impact. Organizations involved in promoting social change tend to have a higher employee engagement, which drives changes in internal organizational structure, strategies, culture, policies leading to improvement in performance and business growth. Women-led enterprises succeed in implementing social change by adapting to dynamic market changes, adopting technology-led implementation, and targeting new consumers and new markets. Learning organizations rapidly adjust to the changes driven by the market dynamics and stay agile to survive and thrive in the marketplace, social ecosystem. These enterprises also adapt to the changing social values, gender equality issues, and women empowerment issues (Stephan et al., 2016). The transformational process of women-led enterprises positively advances on social well-being, framework-based strategic outlook, inclusivity, and building knowledge repositories on innovation-led market practices. Therefore, leaders motivate social change by leveraging innovative market practices to improve the economic growth across developing countries.

Creativity and leadership in women-led entrepreneurial projects have a strategic vision to attract and retain investors and customers. Entrepreneurial education is the key in eliminating social stereotypes and promoting equality through effective leadership. The importance of gender in entrepreneurial leadership is a relatively new concept in the contemporary management philosophy. Therefore, introducing the concept of transformational leadership (Bass, 1985), is based on the interrelation between human emotions, needs, motivation, and engagement to drive changes in the organization and society. However, women are found in an organizational fix termed as 'the glass ceiling', which is referred to as a global phenomenon where women have unjustifiably succumbed to middle and lower-level management positions. Such practice is not only unjust, but also discriminatory toward women managers (Powell & Graves, 2003), which adversely affects the corporate and economic growth. Nevertheless, the entrepreneurial behavior in emerging

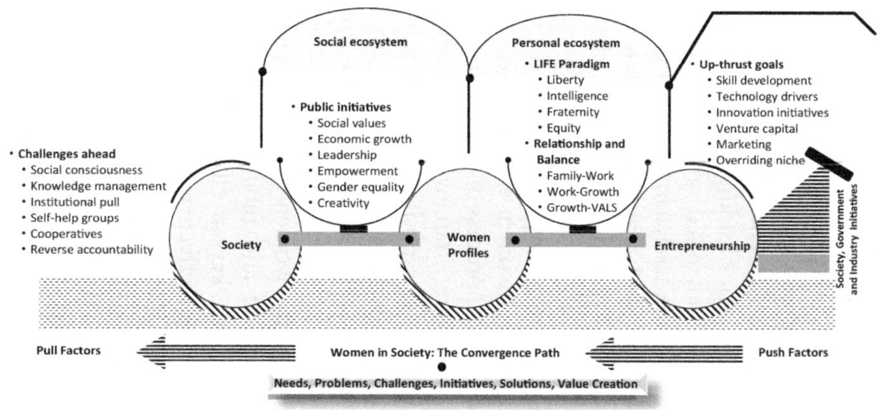

Fig. 2.2 The convergence path of entrepreneurial women in society (*Source* Author)

markets is influenced by the cultural and social practices of the emerging market; however, these attributes may differ by geo-demographic ecosystems. The influence of social attributes on the behavior of individuals and social relations directly affects the success of women entrepreneurs. The attributes of women entrepreneurs such as success-oriented mindset, risk-taking abilities, creative orientation, and search for market opportunities is largely driven by the transformational leadership (Knopik & Moerer, 2008).

In most developing economies, women tend to adopt entrepreneurial practices to become financially independent. The degree of newness proposed by the innovative products and services attribute to the success of the entrepreneurial venture. Women entrepreneurs tend to drive innovation-led organizational performance through clarity in organizational communication, strategic objectives, and rewards and benefits for employees and stakeholders. Entrepreneurs are mainly considered as agents who bring changes in the organizational and social norms through implementation of customer-centric innovative practices. The open management style and transformational leadership motivate employees and drive intrinsic (collective decision-making, rewards, gender equality, and creativity) and extrinsic (customer-centric approach, innovativeness, opportunity exploitation, and cocreation) organizational factors leading to enhanced entrepreneurial performance (Zhao, 2005). Women entrepreneurs capitalize on the operational effectiveness of innovative business propositions through informal social networks (Word-of-mouth), propagation of community values (religious gathering, social events, family reunions), and political outreach (connections or influences to easy bureaucratic processes). Nevertheless, women entrepreneurs tend to accommodate traditional roles such as motherhood within their entrepreneurial objectives to gain social support and acceptance. Hence, public policies need to be improved collectively to support women entrepreneurs and impart training on enhancing the innovative opportunities, building interpersonal relationships, developing social skills, building open communication channels, and integrating cultural values with organizational objectives. Such training will allow women entrepreneurs to examine the effects of centralization or decentralization strategies to attain organizational growth and success. Therefore, management development programs help in increasing the executive capabilities and competencies among women entrepreneurs, increasing the marketability of innovative products and services, which shifts the market dynamics to consumer-centric innovation-driven economy (Idris, 2009).

LIFE Paradigm

Women entrepreneurs face enormous difficulties in their day-to-day dynamics, which can be encapsulated in the **LIFE** paradigm (Rajagopal et al., 2013)—**L**iberty, **I**ntelligence, **F**raternity, and **E**quity. The LIFE paradigm tries to encompass the core values and struggles of women entrepreneurs in their persistent quest to maintain the market dynamics. The business diligence among women entrepreneurs exhibits the attributes of developing streamlined objectives, keeping track of the progress, and carrying out exhaustive risk analysis toward attaining financial independence. However, women entrepreneurs are proactive in sharing ideas on social networks and enriching professional ties, which are imperative in entrepreneurial development. However, women entrepreneurs overcome personal and social difficulties by developing loyalty and trust-based relationship within and outside the organization to promote sustainable entrepreneurial growth. Such fraternity is founded on the philosophy of attaining family-work balance, community welfare, and innovation and technology-led business model, which enables the women entrepreneurs to attain social and financial equity in a long-term entrepreneurial growth. Entrepreneurial growth is a slow but long-term process, where women entrepreneurs find ways to implement innovation-led business model and reintegrate the core entrepreneurial objectives in each business development stage.

Relationship and Balance

The conflict between family and work balance is mainly based on incompliance with the expectations. Such incompliances affect the personal and professional attitude of women in identifying the symptoms of conflict, decrease in leadership aptitudes, and ambiguity. Lack of balance in professional and personal life affects employee engagement, generates emotional discord, and contributes to high attrition rate. The effect of such imbalance is unhealthy for the organization and poses a threat of human capital mobility out of the enterprise, crippling the organization until the matching talent is found and the learning curve is managed (Shankar & Bhatnagar, 2010). The imbalance in family-work ambience can be attributed to time management, stress, and behavioral conflicts leading to a decrease in socialization habits, personal care routines like diet, exercise, meditation, adaptation issues in social arena, and a decrease in marital communication and satisfaction. Therefore, such impact on family is attributed to changes in redesigning the work context (frequent use of technology, odd work schedules, intensifying workload, and entrepreneurial disinterest in facilitating work-life balance). Such imbalance also reflects poorly on employee-work satisfaction, increase in employee turnover rate, and demotivated feeling at the workplace. Apart from changes in the work context, the women entrepreneurs also undergo social changes leading to family diversification, family income-expense parity, and social isolation due to professionally accepted work habits. These changes in social context tend to impact the health of the employee and their family, increasing the cost of healthcare. It is convenient to look at family-work imbalance as an isolated issue, but when it is analyzed in depth, there is a profound impact on the government expenditure on health care system and a tendency of citizens (employees and families) to develop long-term health issues, which can pose a crippling threat to the economic growth of the country. Therefore, the family-work balance is imperative in reducing such crippling economic and social effect with a country (St-Amour et al., 2007).

The concept of family-work balance is not new in the social and entrepreneurial context. However, the implication of family-work conflict among women entrepreneurs has drawn attention to the social deficits. Therefore, the association of women entrepreneurs in multiple roles within the business cultivates meticulous management of financial resources, increased self-esteem, ability to delegate tasks, enhanced social-engagement opportunities. In addition, the dynamic changes in consumer needs and consumer perceptions have given rise to niche-based enterprises and entrepreneurial attention toward bottom of the pyramid consumer segments. These changes have promoted women employees and women entrepreneurs who are willing to outperform their male counterparts (Greenhaus et al., 2003). Therefore, it can be argued that the women-led entrepreneurial growth is slow but sustainable. However, the influence of value and lifestyle (VALS) on the entrepreneurial growth cycle depend on consumer behavior, adaptation of technology, communication of innovative products and services, and influence of entrepreneurial mindset on social trends. The gap in VALS is attributed to consumer behavior and the psychographic analysis of consumer profiles in order to develop consumer-centric strategies, customer-oriented business policies, and customer-oriented product portfolio (Kenney & Weinstein, 2010). Hence, women-led enterprises tend to develop strategic alliances to fill the existing gap in VALS.

Strategic alliances significantly affect the market performance of the entrepreneurial ventures. However, it is important to consider that the entrepreneurial ventures need to maintain an optimum number of alliances, as an increase in strategic alliances would negatively affect the performance of these businesses (Moghaddam et al., 2016). Besides developing strategic alliances, women-led enterprises focus on people-oriented leadership, where the organizational structure is based on developing and maintaining an open relationship with the employees and stakeholders. People-oriented style encourages women entrepreneurs to develop respect, trust, open communication, and engagement, and motivate the employees to outperform the expectations. Women entrepreneurs, who functionalize business model through planning tasks, developing strategies, and setting objectives for their teams and organization, have significant impact on employee engagement and satisfaction. Such leadership style motivates employees to comply with their professional obligations and commitment to improve employee performance leading to enhanced entrepreneurial performance and growth (Chong et al., 2018). As discussed previously, in most emerging markets, women entrepreneurs find themselves at a disadvantage as compared to their male counterparts due to cultural expectations and increase in gender gap. The public policies implemented by the government in the developing countries often face inadequate financing facilities for women-led entrepreneurial ventures contributing to the increased gender gap.

Most entrepreneurial ventures face resource limitations and financial challenges; however, women-led enterprises face financial difficulties such as complex terms of credit rejections of credit applications due to lack of collaterals, lack of financial knowledge, high interest rates, administrative complexities in application procedure, and operational impediments (Quinian & VanderBurg, 2016). More than cultural limitations, women entrepreneurs tend to restrain themselves in managing the enterprises due to lack of self-confidence, fear of failure, and lack of quality time due to unequal distribution of domestic workload. In most emerging markets, microfinance institutions have tried to fill in the gap created by financial market institutions. These microfinance institutions charge high interest rate in a short period of time, leaving women entrepreneurs with squeezed opportunities to seek financial support for their business ventures. However, irrespective of the challenges faced by women entrepreneurs in emerging markets, most financial institutions do not perceive gender as an issue. Hence, no priority is given to gender-based issues leaving the financial institutions perplexed on the question as why women entrepreneurs are unable to find adequate financial solutions (Arnold & Gammage, 2019). Also, financial institutions in emerging markets find it difficult to analyze the biases embedded in their culture due to the lack of female decision-makers within these institutions in order to support women-led entrepreneurial ventures.

Women entrepreneurs also face challenges in securing financial funds due to high credit risk, transaction costs, low returns on investment, and limited exit options in case of failures leading to a mismatch between investor expectations and impact on the society. In most emerging markets, there already exists a gender gap in reference to ownership of fixed asset or property, which acts as a barrier in the financial credit authorization process (Mohammadi & Shafi, 2018). Despite the barriers faced by female entrepreneurs, emerging market that promote entrepreneurial ventures are able to improve the attributes that drive the empowerment of women in financial ambiance. The diversity in the women-led entrepreneurial ventures increases the risk appetite of financial institutions leading to an increase in the gender gap in the society. By implementing the public policies effectively, government can bridge the gender gap. These policies would need to focus on development of a comprehensive gender inclusion strategy toward investors, financial institutions, and market players (Akter et al., 2019).

Push and Pull factors

Like any new business venture, women-led enterprises need to adopt four skill sets comprising cognitive skills, social skills, technical skills, and management skills. Entrepreneurial know-how is reflected upon cognitive skills such as creativity, identification of opportunities, and the capacity to resolve identified problems, whereas the social skills highlight the clear communication ability, employee engagement, motivation, and teamwork capabilities. The social and cognitive skills drive the entrepreneur's ability to achieve business objectives and capacity to learn from the market practices to promote entrepreneurial performance and growth. Women entrepreneurs should also be able to develop technical skills to understand and guide the technological enhancements in the organizational platforms. Technical skills would ease the knowledge-integration process between the various management levels within the organization. The management skills would enhance the strategy implementation process and guide the entrepreneur toward business development process including stakeholders and customers. These skills are necessary for understanding the market-oriented and innovation-led mechanisms (Sousa & Almeida, 2014). The push factors for new business ventures include developing and promoting frugal innovative products and services mainly through crowdsourcing opportunities. Emerging enterprises that launch frugal innovative offer with bricolage attributes aim at underserved consumer segments. Offering such affordable products and services help in maintaining the sustainable component of the entrepreneurial venture attracts consumer attention toward the business offerings. Women entrepreneurs emerge to the limelight from the grassroots of society with limited entrepreneurial education, technological constraints, and resource constraints, yet with capabilities to understand the latent and incipient consumer needs. Such capabilities drive the rate of entrepreneurial success through frugal- and reverse innovation-led products and services (Hossain, 2020).

Social consciousness is also referred to as generating awareness in the society, which is deeply rooted in an individual's consciousness. This core attribute of social consciousness is directly related to the treatment of women entrepreneurs in emerging economies. Social consciousness is also related to the public opinion in the social ambiance, *i.e.*, the collective thought process of the society develops a public opinion leading to acceptance or rejection of certain types of behavior within the social norms (Cooley, 1907). In this context, the public opinion leads to the acquisition and dissemination of knowledge related to the role of women entrepreneurs in the business and social ecosystem. Enterprises acquire knowledge through development of employee skills, training personal, and offering public programs to build knowledge reservoirs (McGrath & Argote, 2000). The knowledge reservoirs are based on resource base view, which emphasizes on the process of optimal use of entrepreneurial resources based on its dynamic capabilities. adequate management of knowledge by women-led enterprises not only helps in identifying, evaluating, and exploiting market opportunities, but also in achieving competitive advantage with respect to the innovation, customer service plans, business process improvements, cocreation, and codesigning strategies. The institutional pull is based on the ability of the government and private sector sponsored programs to attract innovation-led entrepreneurial ventures (Widding, 2007).

References

Abebe, O. J. (2015, December 20). The role of gender in enhancing the development agenda of any country. *Social science research network*. https://ssrn.com/abstract=2847910 or http://dx.doi.org/10.2139/ssrn.2847910

Akter, M., Rahman, M., & Radicic, D. (2019). Women entrepreneurship in international trade: Bridging gap by feminist theories into entrepreneurship and internationalization theories. *Sustainability, 11*(22), 1–28.

Arnold, J., & Gammage, S. (2019). Gender and financial inclusion: The critical role for holistic programming. *Development in Practice, 29*(8), 965–973. https://doi.org/10.1080/09614524.2019.1651251

Auerswald, P. E., & Dani, L. (2017). The adaptive life cycle of entrepreneurial ecosystems: The biotechnology cluster. *Small Business Economics, 49*, 97–117.

Bass, B. M. (1985). Leadership: Good, better, best. *Organizational Dynamics, 13*, 26–40.

Bayeh, E. (2016). The role of empowering women and achieving gender equality to the sustainable development of Ethiopia. *Pacific Science Review B: Humanities and Social Sciences, 2*(1), 37–42.

Blomkvist, H. (2003). *Social capital, political participation, and the quality of democracy in India*. Paper presented at the annual meeting of the American Political Science Association, Philadelphia Mariott Hotel, Philadelphia, PA.

Charlesworth, T. E. S., & Banaji, M. R. (2019). Gender in science, technology, engineering, and mathematics: Issues, causes, solutions. *Journal of Neuroscience, 39*(37), 7228–7243. https://doi.org/10.1523/JNEUROSCI.0475-18.2019

Chong, A. V. N., Lee, U. H. M. S., Ismail, A. B., & Yazid, Z. (2018). Person oriented leadership enhancing employee outcomes. *IPN Journal of Research and Practice in Public Sector Accounting and Management*, 105–122.

Connell, R. (2005). Change among the gatekeepers: Men, masculinities, and gender equality in the global arena. *Signs, 30*(3), 1801–1825. https://doi.org/10.1086/427525

Cooley, C. (1907). Social Consciousness. *American Journal of Sociology, 12*(5), 675–694.

Elias, M., & Carney, J. A. (2007). African Shea butter: A feminized subsidy from nature. *Africa, 77*(1), 37–62.

Field, A., & Tsvetkov, Y. (2020). Unsupervised discovery of implicit gender bias. *Proceedings of the 2020 Conference on Empirical Methods in Natural Language*

Processing (EMNLP). November, 596–608. https://doi.org/10.18653/v1/2020.emnlp-main.44

Gholipour, A., Rahiman, A., Mirzamani, A., & Zehtabi, M. (2010). Impact model of women's empowerment. *International Business Research, 3*(1), 57–65.

Ghosh, S., Applegate, L. M., Ghosh, R., & Kumar, A. (2011). The sandbox: Creating a bottom-entrepreneurial ecosystem. *Case: Harvard Business School*, 1–29.

Greenhaus, J. H., Collins, K. M., & Shaw, J. D. (2003). The relation between work–family balance and quality of life. *Journal of Vocational Behavior, 63*(3), 510–531.

Guido, G. (2018). Voluntary measures, participation and fundamental rights in the governance of research and innovation: Reflections on a 'constitutional' model for Responsible Research and Innovation. *The ORBIT Journal, 1*(4), 1–21.

Guinée, N. (2014). Empowering women through education: Experiences from Dalit women in Nepal. *International Journal of Educational Development, 39*(1), 173–180.

Gupta, V., Hieronimus, S., Krishnan, M., & Madgavkar, A. (2019). *Accelerating gender parity: What can governments do?* McKinsey & Company

Hossain, M. (2020). Frugal innovation: Conception, development, diffusion, and outcome. *Journal of Cleaner Production, 262*(3), https://doi.org/10.1016/j.jclepro.2020.121456

Idris, A. (2009). Management styles and innovation in women-owned enterprises. *African Journal of Business Management, 3*(9), 416–425.

Kenney, M. G., & Weinstein, A. (2010). Psychographic segmentation of the self-employed: An exploratory study. *New England Journal of Entrepreneurship, 13*(2), 1–11.

Khan, A., & Bibi, Z. (2011). Women's socio-economic empowerment through participatory approach. *Pakistan Economic and Social Review, 49*(1), 133–148.

Knopik, M. S., & Moerer, T. (2008). Women leaders and entrepreneurs: Learning from one to teach the other. *Journal of Women in Educational Leadership, 66*, 1–18.

McGrath, J. E., & Argote, L. (2000). *Group processes in organizational contexts*. In M. A. Hogg & R. S. Tindale (Eds.), *Blackwell handbook of social psychology: Group processes*. Blackwell.

Moghaddam, K., Bosse, D. A., & Provance, M. (2016). Strategic alliances of entrepreneurial firms: Value enhancing then value destroying. *Strategic Entrepreneurship Journal, 10*(2), 153–168.

Mohammed, K., Ibrahim, H. I., & Monhammad Shah, K. A. (2017). Empirical evidence of entrepreneurial competencies and firm performance: A story of women entrepreneurs of Nigeria. *International Journal of Entrepreneurial Knowledge, 5*(1), 49–61.

Mohammadi, A., & Shafi, K. (2018). Gender differences in the contribution patterns of equity-crowdfunding investors. *Small Business Economics, 50*, 275–287.

OCED. (2017). *Policy brief on women's entrepreneurship*. https://doi.org/10.2767/50209

Parris, D. L., & McInnis-Bowers, C. (2017). Business not as usual: Developing socially conscious entrepreneurs and intrapreneurs. *Journal of Management Education, 41*(5), 687–726.

Patrick, C., Stephens, H., & Weinstein, A. (2016). Where are all the self-employed women? Push and pull factors influencing female labor market decisions. *Small Business Economics, 46*(3), 365–390.

Pearson, C. (2015). Empowering female micro-entrepreneurs through education: Raising half the sky in just three hours. *Thunderbird School of Global Management*, Case reference no. A03-15-0009, 1–7.

Pinkovetskaia, I. S., Kryukova, L. I., Arbeláez Campillo, D. F., & Rojas-Bahamon, M. J. (2019). Female entrepreneurship: Types of economic activity. *Journal of History Culture and Art Research, 8*(2), 253–265. https://doi.org/10.7596/taksad.v8i2.2153

Powell, G. N., & Graves, L. M. (2003). *Women and men in management* (3rd ed.). Sage.

Quinlan, J., & VanderBurg, J. (2016). *Gender lens investing: Uncovering opportunities for growth, returns, and impact*. Wiley.

Rajagopal, Solano, R., Burgos, F., & Gamboa, L. (2013). The spirit behind Talavera de la Reyna: Angelca Moreno's Pottery. In M. F. Guillen (Ed.), *Women entrepreneurs: Inspiring stories from emerging economies and developing countries*. Routledge.

Rajagopal. (2021). *The business design cube: Converging markets, society, and customer values to grow competitive in business*. Business Expert Press.

Siba, E. (2015). Returns to physical capital in Ethiopia: Comparative analysis of formal and informal firms. *World Development, 68*, 215–229.

Shankar, T., & Bhatnagar, J. (2010). Work life balance, employee engagement, emotional consonance/dissonance & turnover intention. *Indian Journal of Industrial Relations, 46*(1), 74–87.

Sousa, M. J., & Almeida, M. D. R. (2014). Entrepreneurial skills development. *Recent Advances in Applied Economics*, Conference proceedings, pp. 135–139.

St-Amour, N., Laverdure, J., Devault, A., & Manseau, S. (2007). *The difficulty of balancing work and family life: Impact on the physical and mental health of Quebec families*. Institute Nacional de santé publique Quebec.

Stephan, U., Patterson, M., Kelly, C., & Mair, J. (2016). Organizations driving positive social change: A review and an integrative framework of change processes. *Journal of Management, 42*(5), 1250–1281. https://doi.org/10.1177/0149206316633268

Suárez-Ortega, M., & Gálvez-García, R. (2017). Motivations and decisive factors in women's entrepreneurship. A gender perspective in education and professional guidance. *Procedia—Social and Behavioral Sciences, 237*, 1265–1271.

Subramanian, K. R. (2017). Social consciousness and indifferent business postures. *Journal of Advance Research in Business, Management and Accounting, 3*(6), 1–12.

Sundstrom, A., Pamela, P., Yi-Ting, W., & Staffan, I. L. (2017). Women's political empowerment: A new global index, 1900–2012. *World Development, 94*(1), 321–335.

Wang, Q., dtogilvie, & Richardson, L. (2021). Race/ethnicity, place, and art and culture entrepreneurship in underserved communities, *Cities*, 115, https://doi.org/10.1016/j.cities.2021.103243

Ward, A., Hernández-Sánchez, B. R., & Sánchez-García, J. C. (2019). Entrepreneurial potential and gender effects: The role of personality traits in university students' entrepreneurial intentions. *Frontiers in Psychology, 10*, 2700. https://doi.org/10.3389/fpsyg.2019.02700

Widding, O. (2007). Entrepreneurial knowledge management and sustainable opportunity creation: A conceptual framework. *International Journal of Learning and Intellectual Capital, 4*(1), 187–200.

"Women in the Workplace." (2019). *McKinsey & Company Report. 2020*. https://www.mckinsey.com/featured-insights/diversity-and-inclusion/women-in-the-workplace. Retrieved on: 19-May-2021

Zhao, F. (2005). Exploring synergy between entrepreneurship and innovation. *International Journal of Entrepreneurial Behaviour & Research, 11*(1), 25–41.

CHAPTER 3

Gender Dynamics

Abstract This chapter discusses dynamics in decision-making and entrepreneurial operations among women entrepreneurs. It argues the taxonomy of dynamic management in the context of hyper competitiveness, global economic shifts, and the changing customer preferences. Strategies to improve the existing capabilities and competencies among women entrepreneurs have been discussed in this chapter. The collective designing and adaptive marketing capabilities; organizational competencies; and abilities to manage enterprise by sensing new opportunities, capturing values, and transforming management practices have also been discussed here. Discussions on entrepreneurial behavior to accept new technologies to manage creative ventures and develop design-to-market strategies are central to this chapter. The chapter is also focused on feminism in marketing from the perspective of advertising and communication, product characterization, leadership style, and competitive dominance.

Keywords Capability and competence · Technology acceptance · Institutional development · Venture management · Entrepreneurial portfolios

A. Rajagopal, *Women Entrepreneurs in Emerging Markets*, International Marketing and Management Research,
https://doi.org/10.1007/978-3-030-89770-3_3

Gender ideologies in society have evolved over several theses and antitheses over time. Ideologically, the status of women in the society has been argued in the context of economic empowerment, social justice, and human-value perspectives. However, gender ideologies have often been carried away by social and cultural drifts, which have created ambiguity in implementing women's socioeconomic rights and offered justice toward gender equality (Prasad & Thampi, 2021). Since mid-twentieth century, gender dynamics has played a major role in establishing sociopolitical concerns on global platforms, which motivated women entrepreneurs into the social and economic spheres. Women venturing into small and medium businesses have been encouraged to develop creative enterprises and coevolve within the existing social ecosystem. Such stimulation to women entrepreneurs has strengthened their involvement in business with emotional confidence and enabled them to confront negative stereotype ideologies against their participation in social and economic activities. Gender dynamics has transformed the social notions of women entrepreneurs and their leadership traits by compromising the work-family balance and cultural perspectives in a systematic fashion (Deason et al., 2014).

Sociopolitical encouragement in narrowing down the gender differentiation and providing opportunities for women to establish creative enterprises has been effective in the twenty-first century. The number of women enterprises has increased significantly in developing economies by converging innovation with low-cost technologies to stay attractive in the niche markets. Such trend in women enterprises has triggered manifold increase in women work force augmenting local production, expansion of the markets, and reduction in the income gap within the social ecosystem. However, there exists a pertinent question of differential gains among men and women, which appears to be causing an increase in the gender earning gap. Women entrepreneurs with vocational skills constitute a larger demographic platform, which offers relatively lower income as compared to men with managerial skills. Therefore, the gender pay gap appears to be an emerging concern for women entrepreneurs at the grassroots of the society (Barth et al., 2021). Despite the gender pay gap, women at the bottom of the pyramid have made remarkable progress in manufacturing and marketing the customer-centric products by resulting in a clear convergence of human capital investment, innovation, technology, employment prospects, and overall business performance relative to men. Women enterprises in developing economies have largely emerged as an outgrowth of social awareness and ideological push driven by the social organizations and political willingness. The longitudinal and latitudinal studies on gender dynamics reveal that women entrepreneurs have evolved with a new social sub-ecosystem, which constitutes entrepreneurial capabilities, organizational competence, design-to-market, and design-to-value attributes. The merger of sub-ecosystem with principal social ecosystem has created manifold opportunities for women entrepreneurs to collaborate with large corporations and reinforce their entrepreneurial identity (Blau & Kahn, 2017). Most multinational companies have developed several patronage programs to support women entrepreneurs as a feeder link to their branded products and services. Hindustan Unilever Limited, India has pioneered women entrepreneurs' program (*Shakti*-meaning strength in English) by economically empowering them to earn independently by marketing the company's products in rural areas. This program had received enormous participation among rural women, which has contributed to the improvement in value and lifestyle (Reddy et al., 2016). It has been a major breakthrough in overcoming the social orthodoxy about women and their work potential.

The accessibility and adaptability to information and communication technology (ICT) in small and medium enterprises have encouraged entrepreneurs to work with low-cost production processes marginalizing the effects of market competition. Such advancements in ICT have given leverage to women entrepreneurs to strengthen their entrepreneurial potential and establish dynamic relationship with customers, stakeholders, and corporate patrons. In addition, inclusive (people-led businesses) entrepreneurial education has driven economic gains at the bottom of the pyramid by reducing the inequality thresholds in income generation and social justice. Simultaneously, women entrepreneurs have been benefitted with the positive effects of ICT to develop frugal innovation products and gear up pro-customer measures by narrowing down the social consumption dynamics (Asongu et al., 2021). Consequently, the gender effects on entrepreneurship have been encouraging, as several studies done since the fall of twentieth century have shown both aggressive and defensive market behavior for the products and services of women enterprises. Many examples may be cited such as Self- Employed Women's Association, India (SEWA), Grameen Shakti (rural power) not-for-profit organization of Bangladesh, and women-owned small enterprises in Pakistan; which establishes the contribution of women toward economic development and social well-being in developing economies (Kebede et al., 2015).

The modern sociological school of thoughts, in conjunction with the development economics philosophy, has argued several reasons for economic liberalism within gender-sensitive social ecosystem by establishing logical framework for entrepreneurial development. The convergence of sociological and economic thoughts in the mid-twentieth century have surmounted women's contribution in social and economic well-being. Such ideological moves have marginalized the conventional social system concerning the role of gender in the market-dominated economies. Gender dynamics in business has emerged as a new psycho-sociological paradigm supporting the neoliberal economic developments. The older models of capitalism and gender relationship are being gradually transformed as social sub-system models across developing countries (Connell, 2014). Consequently, women have leaped out of the household economy and acquired competence in the entrepreneurial and corporate environment, which is continuously driving equal distribution of income among men and women entrepreneurs in low-income families and high-value enterprises. Such relationship is obvious in the fashion industry, which has adopted ethnic fashion as a high-value product portfolio (Goode, 2010). Women artisans in developing countries are contributing to high-value ethnic fashion products manufactured in a niche industrial ambiance. These niche enterprises have gone virtual today and are catering to the online customers. In Mexico, the artisanal products are largely contributed by women through micro- and small enterprises (Etsy Mexico, Kiki ethnic products, and Lindahermosa Mexico).

Capability and Competence

Capability and competence are considered as principal transformation tools for improving organizational performance. Most managerial transitions are based on improving functional capabilities within organizations and reinforcing incremental managerial competencies to contribute to dyadic organizational growth converging internal and external corporate ecosystems. However, some managerial transitions are more difficult due to leadership ambiguity and unclear organizational goals. The scope and complexity of entrepreneurial performance increases manifold due to leadership and gender biasness. Therefore, women entrepreneurs need to move from a conservative to liberal thinker on one hand, and deliver their services from being a generalist to a specialist on the other. Such transformation endorses the new entrepreneurial philosophy of ***knowing, doing, and being*** within the women enterprises at the bottom of the pyramid. Consequently, women entrepreneurs have been globally considered as the bricklayers to the regional economy and the architects for solving problems. Such socioeconomic transformation of women entrepreneurs has increased their organizational competence and design capabilities to nurture innovative enterprises in upstream markets (Watkins, 2012). The managerial competence can be acquired by adapting to best practices or creating experimental simulations toward business process improvements. Firms with strong managerial process are able to achieve high work performance metrics such as profitability, growth, and productivity. In women's enterprises, the process quality in production and marketing has been found to be weak due to limited finance and access to technology associated with production and operations. Therefore, it is necessary to invest more in improving managerial capabilities as such investments are powerful to achieve market competitiveness (Sadun et al., 2017).

Resource-based view of small firms largely suffer from the mismatch of resources and capabilities. These firms require a pragmatic and rigorous set of competence tests to determine the managerial efficiency and upstream marketing strategies. Women entrepreneurs also succumb to such organizational deficiencies, where they need to move from myopic profiteering approach to strategic thinking toward integrating the competition and industry structure. The core competence in enterprises can be measured from the perspective of competitiveness of innovation, diversification, and profiteering strategies (Collis & Montgomery, 2008). Empowering women entrepreneurs is a socioeconomic perspective, but realizing results from the empowerment lies in creativity, contemporary skills, market understanding, and working with high quality talent and experience. In this context, harnessing capabilities and commitments results in enhancing competence, which is arguably an uphill managerial challenge. Corporate ownership structures, enterprise governance systems, and cocreation programs constitute the fundamental pillars of an enterprise, which synthesizes individual initiatives by integrating people, power, and profit (Manville & Ober, 2003).

Women enterprises venturing into competitive markets with limited resources encounter various social and economic problems such as managing innovations, launching customer-centric products, managing information diffusion on social media, and establishing effective alliances in marketing products. Therefore, successful women enterprises require distinctive capabilities on retail operations alongside the production and operational capabilities to lead in the commercial environment with limited resources (Liu & Ko, 2014). Besides, financial and operational competence, women entrepreneurs require to attain managerial cognitive capabilities, which involves not only capacity building to perform organizational tasks but also activating creative thinking capabilities to underpin dynamic managerial capabilities. Such behavioral attributes help women entrepreneurs in sensing the competition, resizing production and marketing tasks, and reconfiguring organizational design to match the operations at both organizational and customers end. This requires building homogeneous segments in business and contribute to differential performance across competing firms (Helfat & Peteraf, 2015).

Building organizational capability largely depends on the quality of human capital and work culture. One of the challenges of human resources is to match with the intelligence and capability traits in employees, which contributes to culture enhancement, talent application, strategy collaboration, collective decision-making, and implementation. Ideally, these factors improve the capability and competence of entrepreneurial firms. However, in micro- and small entrepreneurial firms, leaders try to be omnipresent and undertake multitasking challenges by delegating less responsibilities to the employees. Such workplace model evolves around leader-centric ecosystem, which hinders capabilities- and competencies-building among employees. As women-led enterprises operate on low capital resources, the above tendencies in managing multilayered tasks are confined to leaders, narrowing the scope of building competencies across employees of different job profiles (Wiseman, & McKeown, 2010). Consequently, in leader-centric task management and delivery practices, micro- and small enterprises often fail in strategic thinking because of distanced organizational capabilities. The distancing in organizational capabilities happens due to lack of trust on employees and the tendency of controlling operations by the entrepreneurial leaders and owners. Often, these firms avoid justifying the performance using organizational matrices, as they are less agile and fail to coordinate their activities across business divisions. However, social enterprises led by women with inclusive business principle aim at developing capabilities and competencies among employees by integrating bottom-up communication and decision-making into the *social fabric* of the firm (Bartlette & Ghoshal, 1990). Figure 3.1 exhibits the factors associated

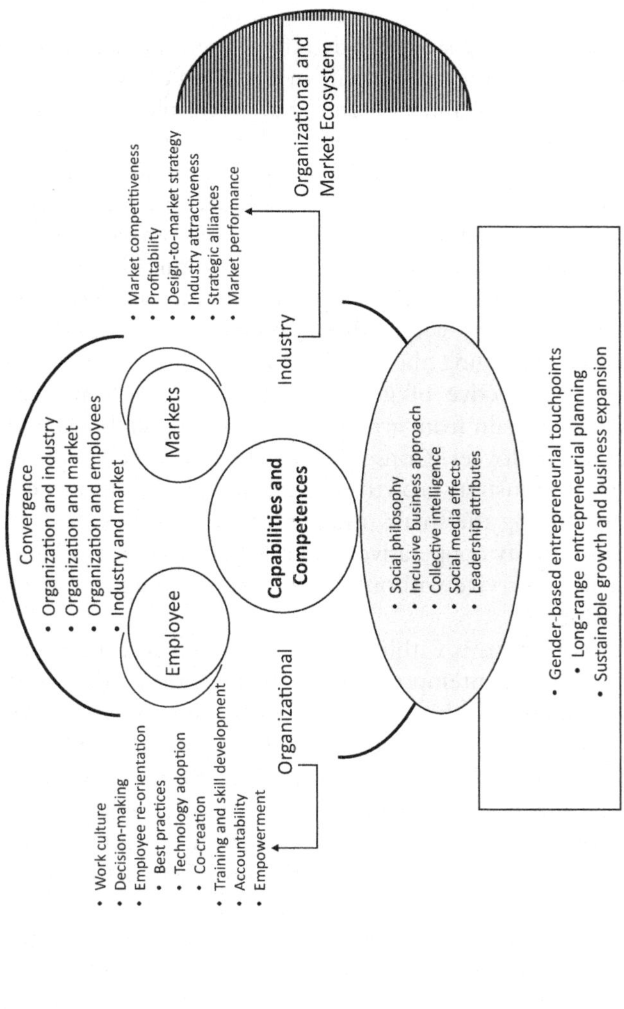

Fig. 3.1 Organizational ecosystem to enhance capabilities and competences (*Source* Author)

with organizational ecosystem affecting capabilities and competencies of employees.

To synchronize the business activities between an organization and industry as illustrated in Fig. 3.1, it is necessary for the firms to continuously improve capabilities of employees and help in demonstrating higher competencies to match with the ecosystems of organization and market. Organizational work culture significantly affects the capabilities enhancement of employees, and reorients them in pro-market decision-making by adopting best practices and contemporary technology, and encouraging cocreation. Therefore, training and skill development constitutes a major challenge in small and medium business organizations. Most organizations evolving out of family business in a niche environment lack in providing contemporary training and skills to their employees, which pulls down the market competitiveness of the firm and diminishes the growth and profitability. Reorienting employees on capabilities and competences helps in fixing accountability within their job descriptions and empowers creative thinking in managing their tasks. As the leaders (or owners) of small enterprises, irrespective of gender, tend to manage multilayered tasks singularly, they refrain from arranging continuous skill development programs for their employees. Consequently, the convergence of organizational goals with industrial growth and market optimization becomes a major challenge among the small- and medium enterprises. Social businesses such as commodity cooperatives and self-help groups working with sustainability projects survive without continuous learning and upstream business enhancement.

An agglomeration of firms within an industry tends to explore design-to-market strategy as a contemporary need to increase market competitiveness and profitability. In this process, firms are driven by the industry attractiveness, which drives them to map the business profile of new entrants and the embedded effect of substitution. Besides, the emerging firms also face the threat of negotiations with customers and suppliers in maintaining the business continuity. However, effective strategic alliances between small and large firms streamline the business performance and open new feeder channels to connect as suppliers with the large firms. The women-led enterprises in the niche market are largely influenced by the social philosophy of holistic growth of the community by generating employment, income, and personal values. Consequently, most women entrepreneurs adapt to inclusive business approach and evolve business through transformative leadership. Women enterprises largely benefit through interactions on social media and collective intelligence, which inculcates the democratic philosophy in operationalizing business. The above gender-based entrepreneurial touchpoints help in long-range planning and ensure sustainable growth and business expansion.

Building decision-making and operational capabilities among employees is the principle needs for the firms to compete in the market and achieve market competitiveness (need). Such dynamism requires business leaders to believe that employees are the roots of organizations, who need continuous transformation (creed). Their business participation needs to be stimulated by investment in training to improve decision-making for contributing to the profit and growth of the firm (greed). In summary, irrespective of the size of business, firms should achieve the competence to manage the *need, creed, and greed* within organizations and in a given market ecosystem (Rettberg, 2016). Low organizational competence promotes conflicts in business operations and develops distrust in the organizational system. Therefore, several social initiatives such as employee well-being, workplace values, and collective social behavior have been adopted in large organizations which believed in delegation of power, tasks, and decision processes. Such initiatives have been observed in south-east Asia and to some extent in Latin America, which have contributed to increasing corporate responsibilities among employees to achieve competitive growth (McNulty, 2014).

Technology Acceptance

Social acceptance of technology is one of the major concerns in improving the production and business operations of small firms. Most enterprises with low capital structure have shown resistance toward technology acceptance as it leads to substituting the human capital in developing countries. Technology acceptance among micro- and small firms has been a major problem due to the threat of mechanization of business operations irrespective of the profit gains. In the textile industry, introduction of power looms has triggered high social resistance and entrepreneurs continued with handloom and pit-loom production operations. The acceptance of technology in low-cost business projects needs high level of tolerance to indifference, rejection, and resistance. Most micro- and small enterprises led by women entrepreneurs face such social dissonance obstructing the business growth in competitive marketplace (Hong et al., 2013). The behavior of women entrepreneurs toward technology acceptance is driven by social media and the collective intelligence through the smartphones. The peer influence and market competition have driven the leader's involvement in transforming the organizational culture by using supportive technology instead of developing dependence on technology. Consequently, the entrepreneurial process is converged with technological, social, cultural, and organizational touchpoints, which contribute to the critical success factors of small firms within niche ecosystem (Morris & Venkatesh, 2000).

Technology acceptance and the age of firm are interrelated as it has been observed that most start-up enterprises tend to develop generic technology instead of adapting to high-value technologies. Upcoming enterprises at an infant age face several resource complexities, which discourages them to associate with new technologies, though these technologies ensure rapid growth in business and in achieving market competitiveness. Such organizational culture is also referred to as cognitive age of the organization, which changes gradually with the convergence of 3Ps comprising perseverance for higher growth, performance, and profitability. The cognitive age of firms influences adoption and continuous use of new technology (low cost *vs* high cost), and motivates firms to develop relationship with exogeneous factors such as comparative growth, competitiveness, and industrial leadership. The cognition of firms (Barak & Schiffman, 1981) may be categorized as feel-age (initiatives on technology acceptance), appearance-age (developing organizational congruence for future growth), do-age (adapting to technology for market competitiveness), and mature-age (thriving for business expansion and attaining technology leadership). Accordingly, a firm evolves with technology across different ages and establishes its credibility in competitive marketplace. Examples may be cited of many companies led by women entrepreneurs such as the honest company, a start-up dedicated in manufacturing and marketing eco-friendly beauty products (cofounder Jessica Alba). This brand is marketed through Costco, Nordstrom, and Whole Foods. Similarly, Tory Burch, the cofounder of affordable luxury fashion brand, has expanded the business with technology and ethnic design arraying handbags, clothing and jewelry as principal portfolios.

Technology acceptance among micro- and small enterprises largely depends on behavioral pattern of customers in the context of perceived use value and the ease of use of technology. Consequently, this segment of enterprises tends to develop customer-centric technology, which is generally homegrown- or low-cost modified technology. The low-cost technology stimulates frugal innovations and focuses on mass customers. Such dynamics is also explained in the critical mass theory and flow theory (Lew et al., 2020). The critical mass theory is focused on expected effectiveness of the group action for social products emerging out of social enterprises (self-help groups, commodity cooperatives, and community business organizations). Individual customers play critical role in accepting technology adopted by micro- and small enterprises, as individual customers tend to induce favorable perceptions among potential buyers as critical mass within predetermined communities. A critical mass of users endorses the state of successful group acceptance by signaling the continuity with the technology under use (Lee et al., 2013). In addition, the flow theory explains the arousal and merriment associated with the use of technology by evaluating its value-based performance. While experiencing the community flow in adoption of technology used by micro- and small enterprises, the community of bias tends to pool contextual thoughts, reviews, perceptions, and ideas to share on social media channels. Accordingly, the acceptance of technology and perceived use of technology are integrated with the customer wallet, which determines the price effects of technology and market competitiveness (Chen et al., 2018).

Technology acceptance is a commitment between entrepreneur and customers to develop product with user-friendly technology to deliver high perceived value for customers. The acceptance of technology in an enterprise depends on its temporal usage (short-term vs long-term), which often makes financial and operational opportunities complex due to the ambiguity of use of technology among consumers. Therefore, it is imperative to explore factors influencing use of technology, decision-making, and customer perceived value for the firms to adapt to new technological ecosystems (Venkatesh & Davis, 2020). Customer commitment to technology is contextual to the perceived ease of use of technology, which refers to the extent of personal belief and anticipated performance value. The perceived ease of use and perceived usefulness are the intertwined cognitions, which encourage customers to accept or reject the technology. Besides behavioral factors, the crowd perception also influences buyer's association with new technologies and alters their cognitive beliefs. Consequently, adapting to new technology is a major challenge in women-led micro- and small enterprises because of low financial resources, low risk-taking abilities, and low growth projections in business

(Taherdoost, 2018). The perceived usefulness is one of the factors determining the customer satisfaction on use of technology. The utilitarian perception of technology generates favorable feeling and contributes to increased satisfaction. However, there exists an ambiguous gap between customer perceptions and desired satisfaction as such cognitive dynamics is influenced by exogeneous factors over endogenous factors. The exogenous factors broadly include crowd influence, shared experiences, and spatial and temporal observations of customers. Accordingly, perceived usefulness may be defined as a combination of cost, time, and risk as an integrated outcome on technology usage (Pham & Ho, 2015).

Institution Development

Women enterprises at the bottom of the pyramid have emerged as an outgrowth of social transformation and are protected within the social ecosystem. These enterprises tend to survive as social brainchild against commercial ventures. Therefore, women enterprises may not have the capability and competence to grow significantly over the commercial counterparts but thrive to cultivate their business on socio-philosophical roots. The women enterprises grow close to social enterprises, which are motivated by the transformational leadership to grow with innovative products and services. Such evolution of women enterprises is congruent with the philosophy of an institution, which are architected as an institution over time (Lee et al., 2021). Women enterprises have gained commercial as well as scholarly attention in view of the indistinctive combination of social and commercial philosophies with innovative market approaches to address social and economic challenges. Consequently, women-led enterprises are evolved with a new philosophical creed of *profit with purpose,* which endorses the commercial economic empowerment of women.

As discussed above, most women enterprises outgrow as social enterprises, attempt to transform the logic of profit-oriented business ventures within the philosophy of social institutions. These enterprises develop reflexivity, entrepreneurial mindset within social ecosystem, and emotions necessary to grow as an institution and conduct operations between niche and upstream market. The women enterprises develop visioning, collaboration, and learning through mobilizing human capital. Such institutional dynamics help them overcome the niche transactions through developing alliances with large enterprises. The women enterprises are largely founded on social values, which build institutional design based on economic, operational, and technological entrepreneurial ecosystem (van Mossel et al., 2018). The socio-institutional approach toward women enterprises is focused on contributing to business growth through different strategic approaches such as peddling in competition, social lobbying, and exploring cross-functional entrepreneurial collaborations. Such transition in women enterprises is sensitive to the leadership traits, work-life balance, and overriding business risks. Consequently, women entrepreneurs working within the social ambit face challenges in institutionalizing entrepreneurial practices, transforming beliefs, setting new business norms, and shielding business against new incumbents. These challenges often restrict women entrepreneurs from developing radical business models by breaking the grassroots and family-based initiatives. The sociopolitical dimensions toward gender-based economic liberty also encourages the move of women entrepreneurs toward transformative business models (Smith & Stirling, 2018). Institutional dynamics of women enterprises develops contemporary cognitive thinking and macro managerial perspectives as an institutionalized rationale to portray a 'big enterprise picture' concerning large-scale and long-term business propositions. Such normative changes help women entrepreneurs to shape their values, beliefs, organizational practices, and operational norms in congruence with the projected growth of business. Accordingly, the evolution of business among women enterprises exhibits enduring features of social and economic life across spatial and temporal dimensions driven by the market competitiveness (Loorbach et al., 2017).

The transition of women enterprises is largely governed by new technologies, industry attractiveness, market competitiveness, and shifts in business ideologies. These enterprises have shown positive growth with capitalistic institutional structure, which allows the enterprises to grow with market challenges. The gradual growth of women enterprises has been experienced through a predetermined economic corridor passing through bottom of the pyramid to niche, and semi-urban to urban market geographies. Institutionalizing women enterprises can be depicted as a storyboard on socioeconomic canvas. The narratives of entrepreneurial journey of women entrepreneurs distinctively establish the path of business transformation, business philosophy, and competitive challenges across the spatial and temporal facets (Boons et al., 2013). The dominant logic of institutionalizing women enterprises can be stated in the context of unilateral push for women empowerment (national, regional, and international sociopolitical dynamics on women empowerment and liberty) as a growing business player with potential economic growth catering to customer-centric touchpoints. A key differentiator of women enterprises is the hybridity in business operations blending social, economic, and entrepreneurial values in contrast with the profit-only business organizations by embedding capitalistic features.

The institutional entrepreneurship can be argued in the context of transformational business system, which encompasses social transformation to gain economic empowerment and overcome the conventional social systems. Therefore, institutional approaches in women enterprises explain individual perceptions, the niche economy, and the interplay between conventional and hybrid business systems. Underlying this multi-level entrepreneurial process, women enterprises become dynamic to shift the patterns of belief, social relations, and market-oriented business practices (Hoogstraaten et al., 2020). Women enterprises that evolve at the bottom of the pyramid can be argued in the context of social-capitalist with liberal business rationale engaged in organizing the entire business process of production, distribution, marketing, and consumption. Accordingly, the institutional phenomenon of women enterprises embodies a holistic view of business within social domain. Such business systems emerge out of social entrepreneurial niche and exhibit dominant business logic to grow in competitive market environment (Feola, 2020). From this perspective, women enterprises illustrate a constellation of features supported by the political, economic, social, technological, environmental, and legal factors (PESTEL).

Venture Management

In principle, venture management encompasses multilayered tasks assimilation with a predetermined goal of the firm. The process of venture management begins with market-oriented or customer-centric ideation, which is derived from shared experiences, conceptual semantics, and crowd cognition. These factors contribute to the ideation process and help in conceptualizing the venture development process through creating prototypes, business models, and organizational design structure. Many firms enter strategic alliances to perform production and distribution operations with specific learning objectives as negotiated with the parent organization. In the long term, such alliances provide scope toward technology adaptation and knowledge management by exploiting effective learning opportunities to develop competitive venture frameworks (Inkpen, 1996). As most women enterprises at the bottom of the pyramid evolve over family businesses, they expand their ventures on the existing organizational design and operate within the conventional workplace culture. With growth in the business, these enterprises tend to enhance the capital structure by exploring the possibilities of venture capitalists (angel investors). Crowdfunding has emerged as a contemporary approach for expanding capital resources, which has played critical role in developing economies by providing donation or equity-based funds to the start-ups. The crowdfunding has widened the opportunities by adding value to the portfolio of women enterprises under structured agreement with investors. Consequently, women enterprises are able to raise their capital and invest in profitable portfolios with the help of angel investors or venture capitalists. Under such financial collaboration, women are able to manage their enterprises by building portfolio-specific entrepreneurial ecosystem within the broad philosophy of inclusive business (Gornall et al., 2021).

The holistic view of venture management process is exhibited in Fig. 3.2, which illustrates that micro- and small enterprises can be managed efficiently across five dimensions comprising venture philosophy, functional dynamics, venture foundations, business canvas, and organizational resources. Most women enterprises, which operate on small scales, abide to low-cost operations and design-to-society as the key philosophies. These enterprises initially carry out their business in niche market and attempt to expand their scale of business by penetrating to the upstream market. They exploit the market ladder based on the expansion of portfolios and geo-demographic outreach over time. Micro- and small women enterprises have a blend of social, economic, and market-oriented concepts within the existing business ecosystem. Accordingly, the vision, mission, and goals are determined by the women entrepreneurs for their ventures of various size. In addition, the venture foundation also requires an efficient resource mapping to manage the functional dynamics comprising production process and operations management (logistics, inventory management, and supply channels). As these enterprises bubble in a niche market, it is challenging to simultaneously develop competitive marketing strategies and customer value through effective customer relationship management. In the process of managing functional dynamics, the innovation and technology play a critical role to ensure the convergence of low cost and high quality to gain market competitiveness and

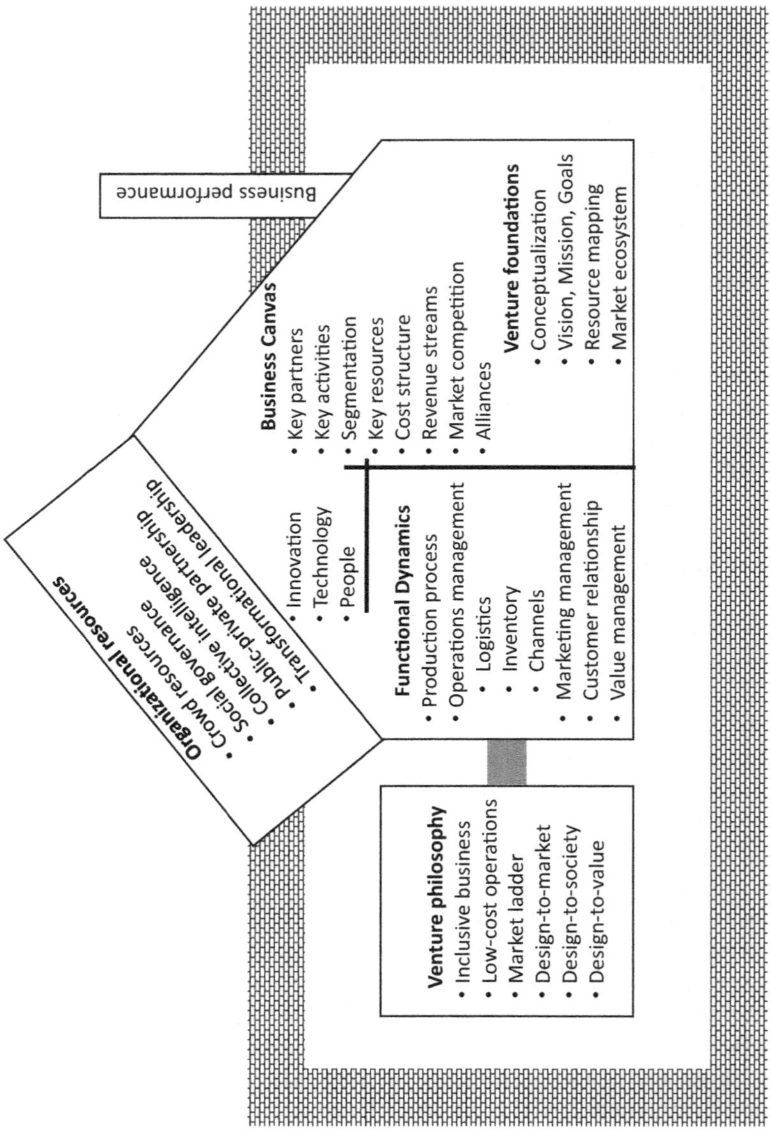

Fig. 3.2 Venture management (*Source* Author)

customer loyalty. However, in the process of venture management at the grassroots, people significantly contribute to guiding managerial process and developing market layout for the products of women enterprises. Such approach attributes to distinguishing these enterprises as the nuclei of inclusive business philosophy as against the for-profit ventures.

Initially it is challenging for women enterprises to develop strategies covering all elements of the business canvas. Consequently, these enterprises develop critical strategies concerning key resources, cost structure, and key activities. With the expansion of business over time, the key partners are identified meticulously in the context of cost–benefit analysis and firms tend to develop strategic alliances to gain market competitiveness and enhance the revenue streams through business diversifications. With the growth of business, women-entrepreneurial firms expand their horizon of knowledge and skills by integrating the crowd resources (crowd sourcing and crowd funding) leading to collective intelligence. As women constitute an integral part of the society, their enterprises have direct or indirect influence of social governance. The crowd cognition and sociocultural values motivate women entrepreneurs to stand with transformational leadership by encouraging employees to participate in decision-making, exercise functional autonomy, and develop relationship with external firms. Such leadership attributes help women enterprises to seek public–private partnership and ensure organic growth and inculcate social responsibility to create social value.

Managing new ventures by women entrepreneurs face several complexities related with work-life balance and cognitive resonance on developing unique business models to achieve market competitiveness and sustainable support from the customers. To achieve differentiated venture management approach, the women entrepreneurs require tangible (bridging entrepreneurial ambitions and domestic responsibilities) and intangible (constructing think-space and arraying ideas) liberty using individual and collective intelligence within the working women's fraternity to demonstrate management approaches for new venture management by attaining the social equity. The tangible and intangible liberty in managing women-led associations have also concerns on ethical perspective of minority enterprises in the society (Smith et al., 2013). The factors discussed above are consciously entwined with the LIFE paradigm of women entrepreneurship, which distinguishes the efforts of women entrepreneurs against the conventional business practices in the society (Rajagopal et al., 2013). The LIFE paradigm encourages women enterprises to combine integrated development logics in exploring appropriate commercial solutions within their competence and capabilities. Though such organizations may face initial fragility, but socio-economic strengths and social empowerment reduces the financial and commercial unsustainability and makes them stronger to stand against the social impacts. The tangibility associated with LIFE paradigm drives rapid advancement in entrepreneurial behavior, which might infuse new dimensions of entrepreneurial innovations including application of digital technologies to gain market competitiveness (Pache & Santos, 2010).

Micro- and small women enterprises largely focus on ethnic value-based products at competitive prices. Such strategy has opened a new front in the campaign of women enterprises embedded with generic or low-cost technologies. In pursuit of achieving market competitiveness, these enterprises largely rely on customer patronage and try to evolve through cooptation (cooperative competition). Women enterprises engaged in manufacturing the fashion accessories with ethnic designs collaborate with large brands as a cooptation strategy and grow alongside of fast-fashion brands (Hout & Ghemawat, 2010). Governments in developing economies with the help of international organizations such as World Bank and OECD, are engaged in delivering training for continuous learning for women entrepreneurs to strengthen their innovative and technological deliveries. In Mexico, such program is being implemented jointly by the Federal and State Governments and World Bank. In five states of Mexico, this program is being offered to analyze its effectiveness prior to the national rollout and is sponsored by INDEM (National Institute of Entrepreneurs). The not-for-profit organization CREA (Crea Comunidades de Emprendedores Sociales A.C.) has been entrusted with the task of training women entrepreneurs in marginalized communities to improve their business capabilities in specialized services (Valerio et al., 2014).

In general, venture management with low resources and conventional organizational design succumbs to several setbacks concerning production and operations activities. Most women enterprises evolve on family businesses in the niche market, and face the problem of overcoming conventional wisdom and adapting to innovative business ideas. Consequently, a large number of women-led start-ups end up with negative returns due to the centralized leadership, lack of team culture, or unrealistic business ideas. These ventures encounter various organizational problems including selection of employees, transforming work culture of the founding team, developing pro-enterprise human resource policies, identifying strategic partners to drive business operations in upstream markets, establish alliances, and attract investors. Such hexagonal entrepreneurial grid often stimulates *false starts* because of non-agile workplace culture and uncertain growth of business. These factors contribute to weak support from investors. It is necessary for start-up enterprises to conduct thorough research on customer needs before implementing the business ideas and testing products at the low-end markets. Most start-ups initiated by women entrepreneurs also face the market research constraints, which triangulates production in business operations, customer values, and market competitiveness (Eisenmann, 2021).

Entrepreneurial Portfolios

The changing taxonomy of entrepreneurs and enterprises have exhibited various entrepreneurial portfolios encompassing innovative production and business operations. The foundation of entrepreneurial portfolios is built through creative construction, market dynamics, and sustained innovation. Therefore, entrepreneurial portfolios have shown the convergence between large organizations and small entrepreneurial firms as feeder channels. Creative construction emphasizes redesigning an enterprise in accordance with the dynamic entrepreneurial and market ecosystems (Pisano & Christensen, 2020). The creative construction in enterprises needs to be understood from the entrepreneurial perspective than the for-profit philosophy of an organization. Creativity in enterprises is contextual to organizational culture and market dynamics, which stimulates new ideas and their validation, and determining the scope of new businesses. Accordingly, market-oriented entrepreneurial portfolios are driven by investment, alliances with large companies, and production decisions. Such linear entrepreneurial path leads to lean approach in management by developing the lean start-up methodologies comprising need-based production, pro-market venture capital investment mindsets, and setting up the competitive business development process. Working with such entrepreneurial portfolio needs entrepreneurs to implement innovative ideas at the grassroots and make decisions at par with the corporates. Such entrepreneurial behavior drives agility in leadership and business operations within the organization. However, developing agility in business decision in context to the market dynamics remains a major challenge among the women enterprises at the base of the industry (Kidder & Geraci, 2018).

The entrepreneurial agility is also supported by the networked incubators who provide preferential access in start-ups to explore the potential partners and developing the workplace for commons. These incubators inculcate agile behavior in enterprises by motivating collective decisions, flexible working patterns, and managing the scale of operations catering to mutual goals with business partners. Business incubators Hotbank and Idea Lab are engaged as networked incubators who also provide funding, infrastructure, and basic services to the start-ups with an embedded objective of inculcating a cross-cultural organizational dynamic among the start-up enterprises. Most women enterprises in the semi-urban ecosystem have been benefitted through the incubator services and shifting their decision-making and operational practices from conventional to agile management with strategic focus (Hansen et al., 2000). The agile enterprises can be developed by understanding the process of decentralized decision-making by delegating the task evaluation, outcome projections, and execution approach. However, most start-ups attempt to understand the concepts and benefits of agility on the basis of need in lieu of incorporating agile practices central to organizational work culture. Agile management practices attract venture capitalists to invest in market-oriented production portfolios. The agile businesses are also appreciated by the social evangelists who proactively create awareness and attract new customers to strengthen the business at the grassroots. Agility in enterprises allows acquiring and accumulating resources and capabilities and encourage teams to customize their work processes to achieve flexible targets over the conventional entrepreneurial behaviors (Rigby et al., 2016).

Crowd-based enterprises and self-help groups such as microfinance institutions are growing manifold in developing economies. These enterprises initiate with limited public participation in a niche environment and evolve as large organizations with adequate institutional resources integrating human capital, technology, and inclusive value propositions. The pioneering organization of Bangladesh Grameen Bank has globally induced the concept of microfinance which has been adapted in various developing economies. Such microfinance institution in India known as *Bandhan* (meaning bond in English), which was supported by a Geneva-based investor, has transformed into hybrid organization by adapting to the advancements in information and communication technology and entered into the formal banking space in India. This enterprise has been built with the dual philosophy of social development and for-profit gains within the banking industry. ***Bandhan*** has built required capabilities to be successful as social and financial venture (Dhanraj & Shah, 2016).

Most start-up women enterprises are founded on previous experiences, preconceived notions (assumptions, self-concepts, and adaptation of best practices model), and peer motivations. These factors attribute to raw cognition in conceptualizing entrepreneurial framework and business models. The main challenge in conceiving the entrepreneurial ideas and developing a structured implementation map is toward updating contemporary knowledge and managerial designs through continuous learning. A strategic perception on architecting entrepreneurial business models need to be based on analytical learning from similar enterprises operating within the existing ecosystem. Learning by experience and learning by adaptation to best practices needs critical appraisal of causes and effects in managing business. Continuous learning develops the measures to authenticate the market-driven ideas in view of the incidences of success and failure of similar enterprises within the industry. Authenticity in entrepreneurial business helps in developing unique product propositions, achieving high brand equity, and maintaining pace (first mover advantage) in competitive marketplace. Therefore, women entrepreneurs need to develop the practice of continuous learning to manage marketing products and services and ensure desired business growth in divergent market conditions. Consequently, micro- and small enterprises need to consider setting up learning goals with focus on the experimentation of various business opportunities (Ibarra, 2015).

Market-driven enterprises focusing on both business-to-business and business-to-customer market segments anticipate exploiting market opportunities continuously and develop a structured learning framework. Market learning process in these enterprises includes exploring open-minded concepts, embedding beliefs in business models, analyzing market feedbacks, competitive information mining, and adapting to transformational business processes. However, most micro- and small enterprises face learning disabilities due to myopic business vision and lack of interest in updating knowledge. Such disabilities prevent these enterprises from enhancing competencies and facing the dynamic management challenges (Day, 1994). Broadly, successful enterprises adapt to outside-in knowledge diffusion, adaptation, and implementation practices as a system thinking method to motivate its workers. This process further grows organically within the enterprise through mutual learning process across the employees and leaders. Consequently, the knowledge pools developed through continuous learning in these enterprises help in improving the production and operation processes, market connectivity, and developing inter-firm alliances. Continuous learning makes rigidity of operations as flexible as possible through controlled experimentation and customized knowledge flow within the organization. For every growing enterprise, continuous learning through experience, failure analysis, and creative thinking are the key determinants to stay dynamic and competitive, but these are not always easy to achieve. The major intra-organizational challenges in applying learned knowledge are developing interest in new concepts, overcoming the fear of failure, reframing the risk-taking abilities, and transforming entrepreneurial mindset to potential gains over the past performances. Due to myopic business vision, most entrepreneurs fall in line with conventional wisdom and are driven by the perceptions on destiny without analyzing the contemporary knowledge and its implications in business competitiveness. The organizational learning can also be developed by analyzing the reasons of demand fragmentation, market entropy, and failures of innovation and technology (Örtenblad, 2018).

In a learning organization, visualization of information is imperative to enhancement of collective knowledge, improvement of organizational identity, pooling of learning members, and developing connections with internal and external experts for transforming the conventional wisdom. The continuous learning within or from external sources in an organization helps in growing innovative skills and ensuring creative development to improve socio-managerial abilities and competencies. Continuous learning also helps enterprises to develop collective work culture toward predetermined common goals and improve leader–employee relationship (Senge, 2006). Knowledge management and continuous learning process are symbiotic in an enterprise, which contribute to knowledge creation, knowledge transfer, knowledge assimilation, and sharing and application to improve the existing business processes. These factors evolve around employees and leaders in an enterprise through an organized learning syllabus. In practice, knowledge sharing significantly contributes to continuous learning through informal approaches within organization and across social media channels on the broader ecosystem. The knowledge management is associated with information and communication technology, which contributes to structured learning and core competencies (Centobellie et al., 2017).

Women enterprises at the bottom of the pyramid can evolve as hybrid structures alike social enterprises by incorporating people, technology, and sustainability associated with upstream business models. Hybrid organizations are able to navigate through complex socioeconomic landscape with the support of public policies, legal identity, and social entrepreneurial citizenship. Social entrepreneurial citizenship is associated with ambidextrous policies of the firm focusing on social development and establishing for-profit businesses. In this entrepreneurial portfolio, social entrepreneurs adapt to agile business policies, which enables ambidextrous growth using appropriate technology and communication strategies. Generally, hybrid enterprises at the bottom of the pyramid are supported by both self-help groups (communities) and public policies (government control), which uphold women's empowerment, economic equity, and business leadership. These enterprises grow as inclusive businesses over time and tend to implement social responsibility initiatives within their operational niche (Haigh et al., 2015). The hybrid organizations also entail business alliances toward technology adaptation within the digital ecosystem to improve their strength on scaling business, manufacturing and operations, and customer-centric innovations. Hybrid enterprises connect with large enterprises also to exploit reverse innovation, ethnic fashion, and sustainable services (tourism) at lower cost by creating awareness through social networks and sharing deep insights (experiential marketing approach) into potential customers across communities. Such business framework enables entrepreneurs to establish hybrid value chain. For example, a Colombian manufacturer engaged in manufacturing and marketing ergonomic tiles for home flooring and décor has collaborated with an e-commerce company to provide online deliveries in Latin American destinations and human rights organization 'Kairos' engaged in managing women sales force to reach low-income markets (Drayton & Budinich, 2010).

Hybrid enterprises adapt to systems thinking process for diffusion of communication within various areas of organization, and restructure institutional design to expand the business horizon and explore opportunities alongside real-time competitors. However, entrepreneurs managing hybrid ventures encounter organizational challenges, which make them compromise with both personal and institutional values. The failure in hybrid enterprises is caused due to value-based complexities in long-term decision-making, acquiring authenticity of ideas, leader approvals on collective judgements, and computer-aided decisions to manage competition. Such difficulties disrupt organizational hybridity and increase value-based complexities, which often breach the compromise between social and business performance (Wry & York, 2017). The advancement of information technology has encouraged entrepreneurs to work with social media channels to generate awareness among customers and stakeholders in the crowd, and its impact has been magnified in the marketplace over time. The hybridity in business of micro- and small enterprises converges with divergent user contents, liberal conversations, and competitive advantages to make these enterprises aware of technology-led customer behavior and redesign business strategies accordingly. Consequently, hybrid enterprises integrate people, communication, technology, resources, alliances, and best practices to grow competitive and distinguish their production and operation processes as techno-dynamic (Mangold & Flauds, 2009).

Hybrid social enterprises evolve by converging business and social missions using sustainability-oriented strategies to compete with established companies within or outside the niche. These enterprises often attract customers with unique value propositions based on the convergence of 3Ps (people, profit, and planet), which emphasize green economy, ethnicity, competitive dynamics, and global value propositions (welfare marketing, sustainable business, and people-driven strategies, which portray the social citizenship behavior). The competitive dynamics for hybrid enterprises create opportunities for technology collaborations related to production, distribution, and information management. Largely, hybrid social enterprises are managed jointly by customers and employees under the transformational philosophy of the leaders. However, these companies differ on exploiting opportunities due to inefficient knowledge-management approaches (Lee & Jay, 2015).

Though many enterprises increasingly debate over hybrid management options, they fail to integrate the liberal workplace culture, logical framework for decision-making, and managing longitudinal and latitudinal information in deriving technology induced hybrid decisions. To sustain hybrid organizational culture, enterprises need to introduce structured flexibility against liberal work culture to encourage systems thinking, cognitive understandings, strategic guardrails, and stakeholder relationships (Smith & Besharov, 2019). For example, Artesanías de Colombia (AC), has faced the challenge of redefining organizational strategy in early 2007. This organization has over ninety percent stakes of the government with marginal private ownership (approximately 3%), which intended to promote Colombian handicrafts by providing opportunities to artisans who belong to a low-income indigenous geo-demographic segment. Such entrepreneurial goals emphasized ambidextrous policies of doing business (for-profit mission) and contributing to socio-economic development (social and sustainability goals) using low-cost technology to develop ethnic products. This enterprise aimed at crossing the niche boundaries to market its products and penetrate international markets by stimulating customer preferences toward organic and sustainable vogue (fashion accessories). Such ambidextrous entrepreneurial platform leveraged the enterprise to hybrid status and increased market competitiveness (D'Andrea et al., 2015).

References

Asongu, S., Amari, M., Jarboui, A., & Mouakhar, K. (2021). ICT dynamics for gender inclusive intermediary education: Minimum poverty and inequality thresholds in developing countries. *Telecommunications Policy, 45*(5), 1–22.

Barak, B., & Schiffman, L. G. (1981). Cognitive age: A nonchronological age variable. *Advances in Consumer Research, 8*(1), 602–606.

Barth, E., Kerr, S. P., & Olivetti, C. (2021). The dynamics of gender earnings differentials: Evidence from establishment data. *European Economic Review, 134*, 2021. https://doi.org/10.1016/j.euroecorev.2021.103713

Bartlett, C. A., & Ghoshal, S. (1990). Matrix management: Not a structure, a frame of mind. *Harvard Business Review, 68*(4), 138–145.

Blau, F. D., & Kahn, L. M. (2017). The gender wage gap: Extent, trends, and sources. *Journal of Economics and Literature, 55*(3), 785–865.

Boons, F., Montalvo, C., Quist, J., & Wagner, M. (2013). Sustainable innovation, business models and economic performance: An overview. *Journal of Cleaner Production, 45*(1), 1–8.

Centobelli, P., Cerchione, R., & Esposito, E. (2017). Knowledge management systems: The hallmark of SMEs. *Knowledge Management Research & Practice, 15*(2), 294–304.

Chen, Y. M., Hsu, T. H., & Lu, Y. J. (2018). Impact of flow on mobile shopping intention. *Journal of Retailing Consumer Services, 41*, 281–287.

Collis, D. J., & Montgomery, C. A. (2008). Competing on resources. *Harvard Business Review, July-August*, 1–13.

Connell, R. (2014). Global tides: Market and gender dynamics on a world scale. *Social Currents, 1*(1), 5–12.

D'Andrea, G., Silva, J. J., Raufflet, E. R., & Prado, M. (2015). Artesanías de Colombia, Spanish Version. *North American Case Research Association (NACRA)*, pp. 1–22.

Day, G. S. (1994). Continuous learning about markets. *California Management Review*. https://doi.org/10.2307/41165764

Deason, G., Greenlee, J. S., & Langner, C. A. (2014). Mothers on the campaign trail: Implications of politicized motherhood for women in politics. *Politics, Groups, and Identities, 3*(1), 133–148.

Dhanaraj, C., & Shah, G. (2016). *Bandhan (B): Sustainable Banking in India*. Institute of Management Development.

Drayton, B., & Budinich, V. (2010). A new alliance for global change. *Harvard Business Review, 9*(9), 1–10.

Eisenmann, T. (2021). Why start-ups fail. In *Harvard Business Review Digital Article*. HBS Press.

Feola, G. (2020). Capitalism in sustainability transitions research: Time for a critical turn? *Environmental Innovation and Societal Transitions, 35*(2), 241–250.

Gompers, P. A., Gornall, W., Kaplan, S. N., & Strebulaev, I. (2021). How venture capitalists make decisions. In *Harvard Business Review Digital Article*. Harvard Business School.

Goode, J. (2010). The role of gender dynamics in decisions on credit and debt in low-income families. *Critical Social Policy, 30*(1), 99–119.

Haigh, N., Kennedy, E. D., & Walker, J. (2015). Hybrid organizations as shape-shifters: Altering legal structure for strategic gain. *California Management Review, 57*(3), 59–82.

Hansen, M. T., Chesbrough, H. W., Nohria, N., & Sull, N. D. (2000). Networked incubators: Hothouses of the new economy. *Harvard Business Review, 78*(5), 74–84.

Helfat, C. E., & Peteraf, M. A. (2015). Managerial cognitive capabilities and the microfoundations of dynamic capabilities. *Strategic Management Journal, 36*, 831–850.

Hong, S. J., Lui, C. S. M., Hahn, J., Moon, J. Y., & Kim, T. G. (2013). How old are you really? Cognitive age in technology acceptance. *Decision Support Systems, 56*(1), 122–130.

Hoogstraaten, M. J., Frenken, K., & Boon, W. P. C. (2020). The study of institutional entrepreneurship and its implications for transition studies. *Environmental Innovation and Societal Transitions, 36*, 114–136.

Hout, M. T., & Ghemawat, P. (2010). China vs the world: Whose technology is it? *Harvard Business Review.*

Ibarra. (2015). The authenticity paradox Herminia. *Harvard Business Review.*

Inkpen, A. C. (1996). Creating knowledge through collaboration. *California Management Review, 39*(1), 123–140.

Kebede, K. Y., Mitsufuji, T., & Islam, M. T. (2015). Building innovation system for the diffusion of renewable energy technology: Practices in Ethiopia and Bangladesh. *Procedia Environmental Sciences, 28*(1), 11–20.

Kidder, D., & Geraci, J. (2018). To innovate like a startup, make decisions like VCs do. In *Harvard Business Review Digital Article*. HBS Press.

Lee, M., & Jay, J. (2015). Strategic responses to hybrid social ventures. *California Management Review, 57*(3), 126–147.

Lee, I. H., Kim, S. M., & Green, S. (2021). Social enterprises and market performance: The moderating roles of innovativeness, sectoral alignment, and geographic localization. *Journal of Business Research, 132*(3), 491–506.

Lee, W., Tyrrell, T., & Erdem, M. (2013). Exploring the behavioral aspects of adopting technology: Meeting planners' use of social network media and the impact of perceived critical mass. *Journal of Hospitality and Tourism Technology, 4*(1), 6–22.

Lew, S., Tan, G. W. H., Loh, X. M., Hew, J. J., & Ooi, K. B. (2020). The disruptive mobile wallet in the hospitality industry: An extended mobile technology acceptance model. *Technology in Society, 63*(1). https://doi.org/10.1016/j.techsoc.2020.101430

Liu, G., & Ko, W. W. (2014). Charity retailing in the United Kingdom: A managerial capabilities perspective. *Journal of Small Business Management, 52*(3), 390–406.

Loorbach, D., Frantzeskaki, N., & Avelino, F. (2017). Sustainability transitions research: Transforming science and practice for societal change. *Annual Review of Environment and Resources, 42*, 599–626.

Mangold, W. G., & Faulds, D. J. (2009). Social media: The new hybrid element of the promotion mix. *Business Horizons, 52*(4), 357–365.

Manville, B., & Ober, J. (2003). Beyond empowerment: Building a company of citizens. *Harvard Business Review, 81*(1), 48–53.

McNulty, R. (2014). Reflections on the importance of business for peace in 21st century peace building. *Business, Peace, and Sustainable Development, 4*(1), 113–122.

Morris, M. G., & Venkatesh, V. (2000). Age differences in technology adoption decisions: Implications for a changing work force. *Personnel Psychology, 53*(2), 375–403.

Örtenblad, A. (2018). What does "learning organization" mean? *The Learning Organization, 25*(3), 150–158.

Pache, A.-.C., & Santos, F. (2010). When worlds collide: The internal dynamics of organizational responses to conflicting institutional demands. *Academy of Management Review, 35*, 455–476.

Pham, T.-T.T., & Ho, J. C. (2015). The effects of product-related, personal-related factors and attractiveness of alternatives on consumer adoption of NFC-based mobile payments. *Technology in Society, 43*, 159–172.

Pisano, G. P., & Christensen, K. (2020). Creative construction: The DNA of sustained innovation. *Rotman Management Magazine*.

Prasad, V., & Thampi, B. V. (2021). Gender ideology and gendered political dynamics shaping electoral fortunes of women politicians in Kerala, India. *Women's Studies International Forum, 84*(1), https://doi.org/10.1016/j.wsif.2021.102437

Reddy, B. V., Rajani, N. S., & Parvathi, A. (2016). Performance of HUL Shakti Ammas in Anantapur District. *International Journal of Scientific and Research Publications, 6*(5), 264–270.

Rettberg, A. (2016). Need, creed, and greed: Understanding why business leaders focus on issues of peace. *Business Horizons, 59*(5), 481–492.

Rigby, D. K., Sutherland, J., & Takeuchi, H. (2016). Embracing agile. *Harvard Business Review, 94*(5), 40–50.

Sadun, R., Bloom, N., & Reenen, J. V. (2017). Why do we undervalue competent management? *Harvard Business Review, 95*(5), 120–127.

Senge, P. M. (2006). *The fifth discipline: The art and practice of the learning organization*. Doubleday Publishers.

Smith, W. K., & Besharov, M. L. (2019). Bowing before dual gods: How structured flexibility sustains organizational hybridity. *Administrative Science Quarterly, 64*(1), 1–44.

Smith, W. K., Gonin, M., & Besharov, M. L. (2013). Managing social-business tensions: A review and research agenda for social enterprise. *Business Ethics Quarterly, 23*, 407–442.

Smith, A., & Stirling, A. (2018). Innovation, sustainability and democracy: An analysis of grassroots contributions. *Journal of Self-Governance Management Economics, 6*(1), 64–97.

Solano, R., Burgos, F., & Gamboa, L. (2013). The Spirit behind Talavera de la Reyna: Angelca Moreno's Pottery. In M. F. Guillen (Ed.), *Women entrepreneurs: Inspiring stories from emerging economies and developing countries*. Routledge.

Taherdoost, H. (2018). A review of technology acceptance and adoption models and theories. *Procedia Manufacturing, 22*, 960–967. https://doi.org/10.1016/j.promfg.2018.03.137

Valerio, A., Parton, B., & Robb, A. (2014). *Entrepreneurship education and training programs around the world dimensions for success*. World Bank.

van Mossel, A., van Rijnsoever, F. J., & Hekkert, M. P. (2018). Navigators through the storm: A review of organization theories and the behavior of incumbent firms during transitions. *Environmental Innovation and Societal Transitions, 26*, 44–63. https://doi.org/10.1016/j.eist.2017.07.001

Venkatesh, V., & Davis, F. D. (2000). A theoretical extension of the technology acceptance model: Four longitudinal field studies. *Management Science, 46*(2), 186–204.

Watkins, M. D. (2012). How managers become leaders. *Harvard Business Review.*

Wiseman, L., & McKeown, G. (2010). Bringing out the best in your people. *Harvard Business Review, 88*(5), 117–121.

Wry, T., & York, J. G. (2017). An identity based approach to social enterprise. *Academy of Management Review, 42*, 437–460.

CHAPTER 4

Women Entrepreneurs in Business

Abstract This chapter discusses the entrepreneurial process through creativity and exploring opportunity, which influences entrepreneurial abilities to manage new enterprises. The success of women entrepreneurs in business depends on customer-centric business modeling. This perspective has been discussed in the context of entrepreneurial creativity, opportunity recognition, and resource management. Entrepreneurial business modeling has been discussed by emphasizing marketing competitiveness, innovation and technology, cost-time-risk factors, voice-of-customer, and critical-to-quality functions. The chapter concludes with a discussion on the role of strategic alliances to improve the business performance of enterprises led by women.

Keywords Exploring opportunities · Business modeling · Resource management · Business complexity grid · Strategic alliances

In the contemporary ecosystem of information and communication technology, there are enormous entrepreneurial opportunities at various levels of market spanning from premium markets to the downstream markets at the bottom-of-the-pyramid. Digitalization and diffusion of communication has enhanced the digital ubiquity, which has expanded business-to-business and business-to-consumer connectivity through crowdsourcing

A. Rajagopal, *Women Entrepreneurs in Emerging Markets*, International Marketing and Management Research,
https://doi.org/10.1007/978-3-030-89770-3_4

and collective intelligence. Social media channels have emerged as the psychodynamic sensors in connecting the critical mass of customers and exploring business opportunities and threats. Consequently, the digital transformation and connectivity grid have helped micro and small enterprises to expand their outreach to potential customers and to the promising markets across geo-demographical segments. Many large companies such as General Electric, has high capital initiative as an industrial network by adding digital sensors to their operational platforms connecting them through cloud-based software to critical mass consumers. Such innovative diffusion process of information and communication has contributed to Big Data, which helps in improving organizational capabilities and competencies. Developing analytical business skills and integrating collective knowledge through crowd-based platforms are the essential elements in contemporary. Such platforms have also helped micro, small, and medium enterprises to connect with potential customers, develop new ideas, and derive collective opinion on business modeling (Iansiti & Lakhani, 2014).

Women entrepreneurs can expand their horizon to explore SMART opportunities comprising the attributes of *strategic* orientation, *measurable* initiatives, *accessibility* to resources and technology, measuring *returns on investment*, and driving *transformation* from conventional to contemporary practices. These enterprises may explore business opportunities in a holistic manner with SMART attributes and get connected to the market with their products and services. Such SMART ways to explore business opportunities, establish connectivity, and experiment with business operations in a competitive marketplace provide new functionality in business, which cut across transcending traditional entrepreneurial boundaries. These enterprises need to rethink business designs over the family firm practices and operate in a niche with value-based business scaling to attract new customers and explore alliances with other companies on marketing, technology sharing, and manufacturing. Consequently, the innovative products with small attributes drive new strategic choices for companies and customers both. These enterprises can create value with SMART attributes to secure competitive advantage, develop new capabilities to withstand market competition, and reach an early breakeven point in business to sustain market competition. Therefore, systematically evolved women enterprises with strategic outlook are able to sustain not only the market competition, but also the emerging threats from disruptive products (Porter & Heppelmann, 2014).

Crowdsourcing and collective intelligence has widely supported the evolution of micro and small enterprises of various portfolios across products and services. The diffusion of knowledge has been channelized through social media, which helped enterprises to connect directly with the customers and transform the social work cultures into business practices. These enterprises gained social sympathy for their products and services, which has helped in establishing a value-based brand culture to attract customers and motivate culture-led market innovations. Accordingly, most women enterprises at the bottom-of-the-pyramid have emerged as the fusion of family business perspectives and crowd cultures, which encouraged cultural branding for the products of women enterprises (Holt, 2016). For example, Glossier, a direct-to-consumer beauty products company (2014), expanded to a large company outgrowing a seed venture managed by women entrepreneur Emily Weiss (CEO and Founder of Glossier). This company has been highly benefitted with the accumulation of social values and aimed at developing personal style as fashion. The initial business idea, business model, and the business practice have been evolved by interviewing several women who wanted to overcome the conventional beauty paradigm and grow with individual identity. The documentation of perceptions of women contributed to the collective intelligence to the company and helped in developing thoughtful designs enabling conversations with women on applying beauty products and inculcating anthropomorphic beliefs with the psychology of objectification.

Exploring Opportunities

Exploring new opportunities among women entrepreneurs is largely influenced by entrepreneurial drivers encompassing knowledge and skills, and the abilities to innovate and manage sustainable business models. Micro and small enterprises tend to counter the entrepreneurial challenges by improving sociocultural business models to thrive in a competitive environment and focus on frugal innovation products. Initially, women enterprises at the bottom-of-the-pyramid contribute to deriving satisfaction among consumers with low-priced products, which provide the social comparative benefits. These entrepreneurial approaches address marketing of low-priced products, minimalistic consumerism, and shared values to reduce the gap between comparative contours and furrows of high-value consumers and consumers of the downstream markets. The entrepreneurial dynamics of social and sustainable business model widely focus on frugal innovation, niche operations, and delivering relative values (as compared to upstream social-consumer perspective). Such micro and small enterprises are initially resource-intensive, based on localized business opportunities, and deliver affordable value to the consumers. Consequently, women enterprises founded on social platforms catering to downstream markets often function with low business dynamics and have relatively shorter business lifecycle (Todeschini et al., 2017).

Micro and small enterprises are evolving around customer-centric business by exploring creative opportunities to provide a competitive advantage to the stakeholders' and cultivate brand familiarity within niche markets. Most enterprises led by women are focused on developing utilitarian products adapting to the circular economy philosophy and developing low-cost innovative products that are able to set ethnic trends in niche and upstream markets. The examples of such utilitarian products might range from textiles to food products, and from digital applications for mobile devices to basic educational tools. Such entrepreneurial products span social and business-oriented products, which enter the competitive markets as frugal innovative products. The recent business opportunities in ethnic textiles have emerged toward manufacturing organic textile using organic raw material (cotton) and manufacturing process (using organic starch derived from Myrobalan seeds). Customer-centric opportunities can be explored by evaluating the customer preferences and value streams to provide comparative gains across competitive products. The products evolved through collective intelligence, social experience, the cultural pedigree of social enterprises, and radical innovations explore new avenues in creating markets across different geo-demographic segments.

Exploiting creative opportunities in micro and small enterprises leads to developing new consumer communities in various socioeconomic sectors, which tend to promote ethnic vogue, cultural diversification, and profit with purpose marketing opportunities for innovative products. Such consumer communities are identified in the upstream (premium consumers) and downstream (mass and bottom-of-the-pyramid consumers) who prefer to get associated with ethnic fashion and price advantages for utilitarian products, respectively. Such creative enterprises lead to developing specific ventures with specialization in artistic and creative products within socioeconomic stability in business. Exploring creative ideas by women entrepreneurs enables them to bring together social, public, and private resources for developing integrated business models to exhibit innovative prototypes. Creative enterprises face high market uncertainty and usually penetrate the market without evaluating the market demand, the intensity of competition, and consumer preferences. Consequently, creative enterprises with innovative products live short market lifecycle and succumb to the organized market structure and operation processes. However, creative enterprises are based on continuous learning and are able to generate sustainable customer values and solutions to the existing needs with affordable prices. The entrepreneurial creativity is a great stimulant to organizational innovation and low-end market effectiveness, and serve consumer preferences within market niche (Chang & Chen, 2020).

In developing countries, business opportunities for women entrepreneurs is largely supported as an institutional action through coordinated activities of the community, social leaders, and entrepreneurs. Such institutions help women achieve economic empowerment and overcome organizational resource gaps (finance, human resources, technology, and production management), and develop competencies through an integrated approach. Association of Lady Entrepreneurs of Andhra Pradesh (ALEAP), an institution in southern India, has helped women entrepreneurs in acquiring competencies and capabilities to improve productivity and market competitiveness through various phases. This institution has established more than two industrial estates for women entrepreneurs with a focus on improving the financial and manpower constraints in enterprises to streamline the manufacturing process and improve marketability of their products. However, scaling up operations and exploring new opportunities have always been entangled with the cultural and personality attributes of entrepreneurs. The institutions like ALEAP have largely served as the incubators for promoting women entrepreneurship and evolved growth strategies by converging stakeholders and other market players in the entrepreneurial ecosystem (Avadhanam & Pidikiti, 2014).

Women entrepreneurs face various socioeconomic challenges in exploring an appropriate business idea to integrate into the existing or new ventures. Generating new idea may not be a major constraint for women entrepreneurs but analyzing the economic viability and technological feasibility in implementing the ideas and concepts often lack clarity. However, liberal thinking matched with the knowledge, aptitude, and practice-oriented behavior helps women entrepreneurs to develop firm concepts on business ventures. Most women entrepreneurs depend on family and fraternity who help in shaping their ideas and provide strengths to overcome the social and cultural stigmas. Women entrepreneurs are often hesitant to architect their ideas and transform them into a successful business venture due to lack of confidence and social equity concerns. Consequently, women entrepreneurs require persistence, clarity in venture blueprint, and the ability to analyze the business growth of ventures. However, pressures from the social behavior to build managerial skills and work with the social networks often hinder the progress of new ventures led by women entrepreneurs. Women enterprises tend to survive at niche levels with innovative products and services. However, such enterprises may significantly grow over the commercial ventures provided women entrepreneurs get adequate social support to stabilize in local markets and gain strengths in opening the niche for wider commercial networks (Lee et al., 2021). These attributes of women entrepreneurs endorse the core concepts of LIFE paradigm as discussed in the pretext and contributes to the social and personal perspectives of entrepreneurial mindset (Rajagopal et al., 2013).

Entrepreneurs tend to learn new perspectives of innovation, market demand, and consumer preferences, which helps them redefine their entrepreneurial ecosystem and integrate design-to-value and deign-to-market concepts to the core of their operations. However, in adapting to the new product ideas from the market competition, the cost of production appears to be a major challenge though such ideas may have long-term gains. Such opportunities are strategic and require critical functions like product engineering, customized prototypes, and lean manufacturing plan to develop a competitive advantage with innovative products and create value chains. While exploring new business opportunities, micro and small entrepreneurs need to map the capabilities and resources to develop business strategies and explore various manufacturing and marketing choices (Gottfredson et al., 2005). One of the major challenges with the micro and small enterprises as a family business led by women is to optimize costs, enhance market competitiveness, and streamline short-run financial benefits to manage the financial cycle. Consequently, manufacturing frugal innovative products with low-cost technology yield short-run and bottom-line returns, which is often viewed as a niche opportunity with possibilities of creating lower value chains. Most women enterprises begin their entrepreneurial journey by designing ethnic and sustainable products. These enterprises operate on innovative business models but are confined to niche markets, as they fail to create wider business platforms to facilitate marketing operations and customized transactions (Nidumolu et al., 2009).

Micro and small enterprises often conduct business with cognitive motivation and emotions rather than evaluating the success or failure of business projects. Therefore, innovations for consumer products are largely associated with entrepreneurial traits, emotions, experiences, and cognitive abilities as compared to the key factors portrayed in the business canvas. Entrepreneurs at the bottom-of-the-pyramid explore business opportunities within conventional scenarios, though the contemporary market trends offer attractive business propositions. Often entrepreneurs possess an outlook of low-risk and sustained business, which confines them to niche market. Consequently, small firms are unable to bag big opportunities and respond to major market shifts by capitalizing on existing opportunities (Christensen & Overdorf, 2000). Creative small enterprises may also explore the business-to-business alliances with large companies and establish feeder connections for providing semi-processed raw materials or unbranded finished ethnic products. Entrepreneurs engaged in manufacturing ethnic silk products in Southeast Asia including India, Bangladesh, and Sri Lanka serve as the feeder channel to export firms. However, the terms of reference of these enterprises are contractual and the innovative tasks are synchronized with the international market demand. In many developing countries, the APEX organizations managed by the government streamline the production and supply operations of individual entrepreneurs connected with a registered social body or cooperatives. Though the business-to-business operations of micro and small entrepreneurs reflect complex operations, they can be simplified with experienced managerial talent through distinctive business stages and symmetric operational processes (Gulati et al., 2008).

The new market challenges are encouraging micro and small enterprises to transform the enterprises with new technology to meet the market demand and consumer preferences. The e-commerce has emerged as a contemporary conundrum influenced by crowd behavior, shifts in consumer preferences, and reduction in transaction costs. Accordingly, emerging enterprises are aiming to digitalize their business operations and transform the conventional business philosophy. Women entrepreneurs in many developing countries including India, Bangladesh, Thailand, China, and South Korea in Asian region, and Mexico in the North

American region have rebooted their businesses to ambidextrous platforms: brick-and-mortar stores and e-commerce. Most artisanal products including fashion accessories and apparel blended with ethnic values and designs are being pushed through various e-commerce channels. Technology oriented microenterprises associated with Fintec have focused on developing a digital application for augmented reality, genomics, and simulations to support the digital business of large companies. These enterprises develop new ideas or borrow ideas through crowdsourcing, and create consumer value after relentless experimentation. This entrepreneurial process may be defined as a parallel business play, which develops convergence of local–global markets by establishing a feeder link with large commercial firms (McDonald & Eisenhardt, 2020). The emerging perspectives on digitalization of micro and small enterprises are driven by customer engagement, development of cyber-physical production systems, and redesigning enterprise architectures. Digitalization of enterprises is positively related to financial performance. The use of social media also influences entrepreneurs to transform their business models through digital platforms, which helps in reducing marketing costs and improving customer relations. Adopting digital technologies helps in improving value propositions and the scale of business with agility, and exploring new business opportunities to overcome the infrastructural and logistics resource constraints. Digitalization of enterprises is a continuous process in a phased manner contextual to resources, entrepreneurial design, growth strategies, performance metrics, and goals (Eller et al., 2020).

Digitalization in micro and small enterprises are more helpful in reducing the transaction costs and improving economic advantages for the firms, which are serving as the supplying feeder channels to large companies. Computer-aided operations in these enterprises reduce the cost, time, and risk complexities, which augments the possibilities of narrowing down the time of order processing, associated risks in delivery, and overrun of costs as observed in manual operations. Digitalization of business operations enhances supplier attractiveness by improving financial factors, strategic relationship, and value and trust to develop partnership and expanding business through relationship specific investments. Though the partnering attractiveness of suppliers is higher in offline or face-to-face interactions such as in-person negotiations; online tools, and online media resources like interactive websites and social networks have become critical to the success of micro and small enterprises (Tóth et al., 2020).

Business Modeling

The conventional business models commonly adopted by entrepreneurs include managing low-resource firms having short-term goals and are based on marginal profit propositions, as against the contemporary business philosophy of strategic goals with value-based profiteering approach. However, these entrepreneurs are gradually adapting to profit-with-purpose approach for enhancing business performances by creating value continuum. Business models by nature are designed not to change, which is very common with micro and small enterprises. Consequently, these enterprises become less flexible to changing operational requirements and resistant to adopting new managerial practices. The transformation in business model takes time for the enterprises to adapt, as this process is affected by exogeneous factors to a large extent. In addition, the organizational culture, employees' willingness to accept changes in the business process, and reorganizing decision hierarchy within the organization are the key elements in improving the entrepreneurial performance. Consequently, interdependencies across endogenous and exogeneous factors slow down the transformation process, as the business units increasingly ingrain the operational complexities by tasks and by nature of the industry. Business model is a transaction process including backward and forward linkages from manufacturing to marketing, and sales to value creation. However, it is considered as a conventional journey from entrepreneurs to consumers, and firms need to develop the convergence of divergent factors encountered in such a business path. It is necessary for entrepreneurs to leverage continuous learning to support each stage of the entrepreneurial business journey with specific types of innovation, which synchronizes interdependencies in the business process yielding to the optimal set of performance matrix (Christensen et al., 2016).

Women entrepreneurs and the founding managers have always gone a mile ahead in transforming the conventional business models to contemporary and customer-centric models by inducting customer lifetime value atop of the performance matrix combined with digitalization process. Oregon (USA)-based clothing company Wildfang focused on fashion apparel and accessories, which inspired menswear trends with a radical brand built around *badass tomboy* image. Emma Mcilroy, the CEO of

Wildfang developed the performance matrix based on customer lifetime value. The tools for measuring performance of the company in a given market scenario included convergence of customer lifetime-value modeling with business canvas. Accordingly, the company built strategies around bricks and clicks with a multi-sided and omnipresent fashion platform (Mathwick, 2017). Successful entrepreneurial business models are associated with internal capabilities and external relationships to develop an integrated approach with the business-design cube comprising categorical strategies of design-to-market, design-to-society, and design-to-value (Rajagopal, 2021). Emerging micro and small enterprises can choose to operate as feeder enterprises, omnichannel enterprises, modular producers, and sustainable enterprises with specific business models. In view of the appropriate selection of options, these enterprises need to evaluate opportunities and threats to reaffirm their new business options and future connections with dynamic business ecosystems. However, the micro and small enterprises need to safeguard their business operations from growing digital disruptions, cannibalization, and complex business ecosystems. Therefore, these enterprises need to be specific on their business operations, and in developing control standards to create sustainable value chain. It has been observed that these enterprises generally have a narrow focus on building value chains against mainstream competitors to gain psychosocial advantage of consumers and trigger organic entrepreneurial growth (Weill & Woerner, 2015).

Business modeling in micro, small, and medium firms is largely an unorganized process, as these enterprises run their business operations on experiential practices than adapting to innovative and competitive strategies learnt from the contemporary business ecosystem. However, the business modeling process in large firms follows a structured pattern, unlike the radical outlook of emerging enterprises irrespective, of their scale of business. Therefore, it is necessary for the enterprises to draw a roadmap of business model to support managerial decisions in view of business innovations, competitive dynamics, and the changing customer-centric strategies. It has been observed that most micro and small enterprises adapt to repeatable business models instead of combining best practices around the business ecosystem and internal capabilities and competencies of enterprises (Christensen et al., 2016). As most emerging enterprises invest time and resources in building business models without thinking about the competition, they are often jeopardized by unforeseen risk and uncertainty. These enterprises may have a chance to succeed in niche market with conventional business models due to the first mover advantage. However, it is unlikely to get the same success outside the niche market, as these firms are unable to analyze the extent of the impact of market competition on their businesses. Generally, these enterprises adopt a follower path to develop business model by observing the market challengers and leaders. The innate business philosophy of low-resource-based localized firms is commonly perceived as *winner-takes-all-effects*, which explains the follower behavior of these firms. For example, most start-up enterprises engaged in developing computer applications tend to explore the success path of established companies in the niche, regional, or global markets (Casadesus-Masanell & Ricart, 2011).

Business modeling in micro and small enterprises is considered to be of low priority by conventional leaders due to the traditional entrepreneurial mindset emerging out of the family business practices. It is necessary for these firms to critically examine the combined effects of business analytics (industry attractiveness and bottom-line marketing mix) to gain competitive advantage. Therefore, the business model of an emerging enterprise should be able to establish differentiators, performance indicators, and custom modeling by product portfolios and markets to manage the uncertainty and 'what if' scenarios. These enterprises need to track, analyze, and use inclusive decisions through customer engagement to manage competitive lead and customize the baseline business matrix (Davenport et al., 2010). The effective business modeling can be carried out successfully by collaborative leaders who put connectivity across stakeholders of the firm to make collective decisions. The collaborative leaders use social media and technologies in streamlining the business processes unconventionally without spending time and energy in conventional meetings and struggling to compromise the decisions. People-led business models have been successful to a large extent in both small and large enterprises, which built the business paradigms leveraging diverse talent, ideas, and operational guidance to foster relatively higher performance through collaborative culture (Ibarra & Hansen, 2011). The attributes of entrepreneurial business model in the context of contemporary business scenarios are illustrated in Fig. 4.1.

The entrepreneurial business model is woven around four principal constituents comprising business opportunities, elements of business canvas, attributes of social motivation, and factors affecting market dynamics. One of the major challenges faced by the growing entrepreneurs is to explore business opportunities and identify the

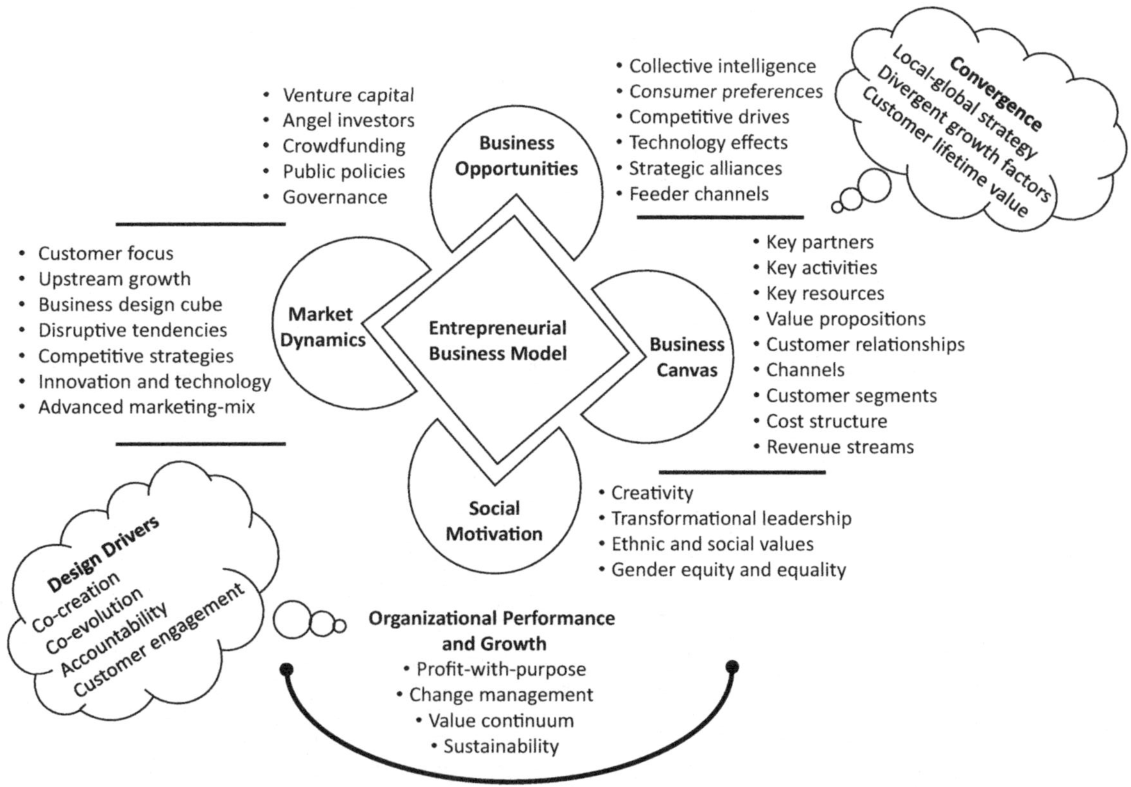

Fig. 4.1 Entrepreneurial business paradigm (*Source* Author)

market-driven and organizational competency-based business activities to develop an appropriate business model. The collective intelligence emerging out of crowdsourcing and crowd behavior combined with the trend of consumer preferences largely guides entrepreneurs to identify suitable business and develop the business model accordingly. In this process, it is necessary for entrepreneurs to track various competitive drives sparked by technology effects (generic and disruptive) and innovation incubators (frugal and reverse innovations). The business modeling process is also affected by exploring strategic alliances broadly in the areas of production, distribution, and technology. Such alliances between micro and small enterprises, and the large firms help in developing integrated business models with focus on conducting business as feeder channels. Strategic alliances are set up for a dedicated function in the aforementioned areas with mutual goals of solving operational problems such as improving the supply chain, inventory management, developing innovative products, and delivering services to support the existing operations infrastructure. The key alliance management needs to integrate knowledge management and external visibility, coordinate between partnering organizations, and develop employee accountability. Exploring business opportunities as alliance with the partnering companies needs to be systematically established to redesign production and operations activities, leverage employee feedback, and share the know-how on technology and specific management issues (Dyer et al., 2001).

Elements of business canvas take the center stage in the development process of entrepreneurial business model. The business canvas integrates nine key elements as exhibited in Fig. 4.1. The above discussed key elements help enterprises in developing strategic customer relationships and create sustainable value propositions across predetermined and new customer segments. In addition, channel management with the objective of increasing business impact in a competitive marketplace to improve the market share and revenue streams is the challenging element in the business canvas. The cost structure plays a moderating role in accommodating innovation, technology, value propositions, and customer relations, and carrying out key activities through the business partners. Theoretically, a business model is based on the assumptions about the elements of business canvas and analyzing the psychosocial behavior of customers and the volatility of competitors strategies. However, steering the elements of business canvas within contemporary practices helps the enterprises in innovating business model by customizing the marketing and services mix, adapting to changing incentives in the value chain, and encouraging reverse decision-making process (Ovans, 2015).

Social motivation plays a key role in developing entrepreneurial business at the niche by inculcating the ethnic and social values in business propositions. The social push in entrepreneurial business is largely regarded as a creativity booster, which is largely supported by crowdsourcing and collective intelligence. In addition, transformational leadership in micro and small enterprises encourages the employees and stakeholders to contribute to creative designing and production process by optimizing the value propositions at low-cost with acceptable technology. The role of society has also been critical in encouraging gender equity and equality in entrepreneurship and business. Market dynamics lays focus on managing preferences of customers for business continuum and bidirectional growth in upstream and downstream market. Accordingly, emerging enterprises tend to focus on the triadic business strategy (Rajagopal, 2021) comprising design-to-market (customers and competitor-oriented strategies), design-to-society (social media-based communication diffusion and social marketing), and design-to-value (strategic customer relations, building loyalty, and co-creation). However, most enterprises operating in the niche market, and initiating their business journey in upstream markets, are often affected by the competitive strategies stormed by unpredicted disruptions caused by low-cost radical innovations (Sutton, 2001).

Entrepreneurial business modeling is significantly affected by financial resource management, which involves fundraising, pooling resources, and funds management strategies. The major challenge in managing entrepreneurial finances can be broadly categorized as venture capital management, attracting angel investors, and crowdfunding. There is an uncertainty embedded in these fund management options (Chemmanur et al., 2011). However, the process of venture capital management and crowdfunding could help entrepreneurs to better cope with the uncertainty of innovations and significantly improve the level of innovation. Angel investors are attracted to potential business models, which could sweep across the contemporary competition. Public policies also help micro and small enterprises in pooling funds and systematic utilization of financial resources in managing production and business operations. Effective business models encourage the convergence of local–global strategy (reverse innovation) by managing divergent growth factors (microeconomic and social factors) and the customer value (lifetime value, and social values). The factors discussed in entrepreneurial business model as illustrated in Fig. 4.1 can be synthesized in four principal business components comprising co-creation (innovation and organizational culture), co-evolution (organizational design, performance, and growth), accountability (employee engagement, empowerment, and decision-making), and customer engagement (psychosocial traits and the sense of belongingness).

Resource Management

Resource management in enterprises has a direct impact on performance management. Managing resources and enterprises is complex, as it involves interdependencies across various internal and external factors comprising finance, human capital management, and investments related to future growth. These factors affect productivity and performance of enterprises tactically and strategically. Effective management of resources in micro and small enterprises affects the speed of business in the context of first-mover advantage, agility, scaling of business, and growth through continuous innovation. Alike financial resources, management of the human resource in deploying high talents to improve organizational performance and business decisions is also equally challenging in the emerging enterprises. The human resource encourages high-quality talent deployment as an intangible corporate investment, which contributes to the development of idiosyncratic work culture to improve organizational performance, value streams, profitability, and continuous growth embedding market competitiveness (Liu et al., 2007). However, the constraints in managing financial and capital resources in micro and small enterprises exhibit major challenges in driving organizational performance. The fundamental financial concepts encompassing fundraising, working capital management, liquid-cash flows, returns on investment, and debt/capital ratio. These attributes of financial management critically affect the liquidity risk, profiteering, and business growth at the nuclei of micro and small enterprises. Consequently, these enterprises largely adapt to short-run management perspectives deployed by the vibrant market- and internal business ecosystems (Welsh & White, 1981).

Low financial resources in micro and small enterprises have been a perennial problem over the years, and across developing countries. These enterprises commonly employ a small proportion of their own capital and explore proportional funds from various sources including financial institutions (commercial banks and microfinance institutions), government subsidies, and crowdfunding opportunities. Lending-based crowdfunding attracts fundraising among these enterprises, which is supported by social organizations and informal entrepreneurial bodies such as self-help organizations besides the push from government programs. The crowd investors are attracted by publishing business proposals on selected blogs advocated by social organizations to generate a collective pool of funds to support start-up enterprises. The crowdfunding emerges in various categories such as donations, peer-to-peer funding, reward-based finding, and equity-based funding. At the microlevel, enthusiastic entrepreneurs try to pool funds within the community by assuring the returns on capital employed with the focus on generating short-term gains and designing the payback offers. However, formal crowdfunding process in many developed and developing countries has been regulated in the context of investors' interest, tax implications, and financial performance of the firm. Consequently, crowdfunding has been brought under the domain of public-funds utilization, and is governed through both social and public authorities.

Micro and small enterprises function largely on creative and emotional intellect instead of deriving decisions meticulously on the profiteering concepts. These enterprises assume that cost is an external factor, which determines the spending capacity on resources (raw material, technology, and production). Consequently, their belief in cost management across diverse product lifecycles is largely based on conventional foundations, and these enterprises fail to implement distinctive strategies on reducing the cost. Hence, the rationalization of cost in various production functions in these enterprises is minimal, which causes longer breakeven points and longer time for investment payoffs. Therefore, cost containment during production and business operations jeopardizes the business continuum and profitability. These enterprises, which opt for adapting to contemporary technology and digitalization of various business processes, tend to lower the costs aggressively. The convergence of lowering the cost, time, and risk factors helps in increasing the product lifecycle, which contributes to achieving consistent performance and market competitiveness (Cooper & Slagmulder, 2004).

Collaborative ventures significantly support new start-ups through providing a structured investment environment to pool funds, and develop an appropriate funds utilization plan for improving productivity and profitability. A venture capital example from Canada illustrates that the selection of potential investors to enhance the capital status of start-ups helps in improving their business stakes with partnering firms and improve their market share and profitability over time. Helarctos Ventures, a seed capital investment fund based in Toronto, Canada, has attracted venture capital investors in the mobile wireless technology industry, which roped in promising start-ups that offered divergent growth perspectives. Each investment in the partnering start-ups was considered as a major decision based on long-term allocation of capital, assessment of time, and projection of potential risks. In this process, experienced investors evaluated and selected opportunities by exploring market trends and vulnerability of cost-time-risk (CTR) grid. However, experience-based insights from investors have helped in stabilizing the elements of CRT grid (Wong, 2019).

The crowdfunding of business projects has been made more transparent to investors and the social development implementors, which provides better options on selection of entrepreneurial business projects, their expected outcome, and co-creation of social values (Rajagopal, 2021). However, few entrepreneurial business projects are built on the grants, largely used as seed capital, provided by the government, corporate sector, and international organizations. In these projects, working capital is managed through various sources including public and private funding as discussed above. There are various elements, as illustrated in Fig. 4.2, that are interrelated in managing financial resources in micro and small enterprises led by socially empowered women entrepreneurs.

Money supply in micro and small enterprises is directly proportional to the production potential and profitability. However, the relationships between money supply, resource utilization, productivity, and marketing are highly volatile; and the optimization of resource-profit association is a complex phenomenon. Broadly, the resources also include raw material, technology, and managerial know-how. Women entrepreneurs often face complexities in resource management due to the rising interdependencies among the above-discussed factors. Therefore, effective government intervention would help in resolving the problems associated with resource management among micro and small enterprises; improving production infrastructure and applied technologies; and proactively developing the product markets by streamlining the money supply in these enterprises (Adams et al., 2019). Crowdfunding is attracted by

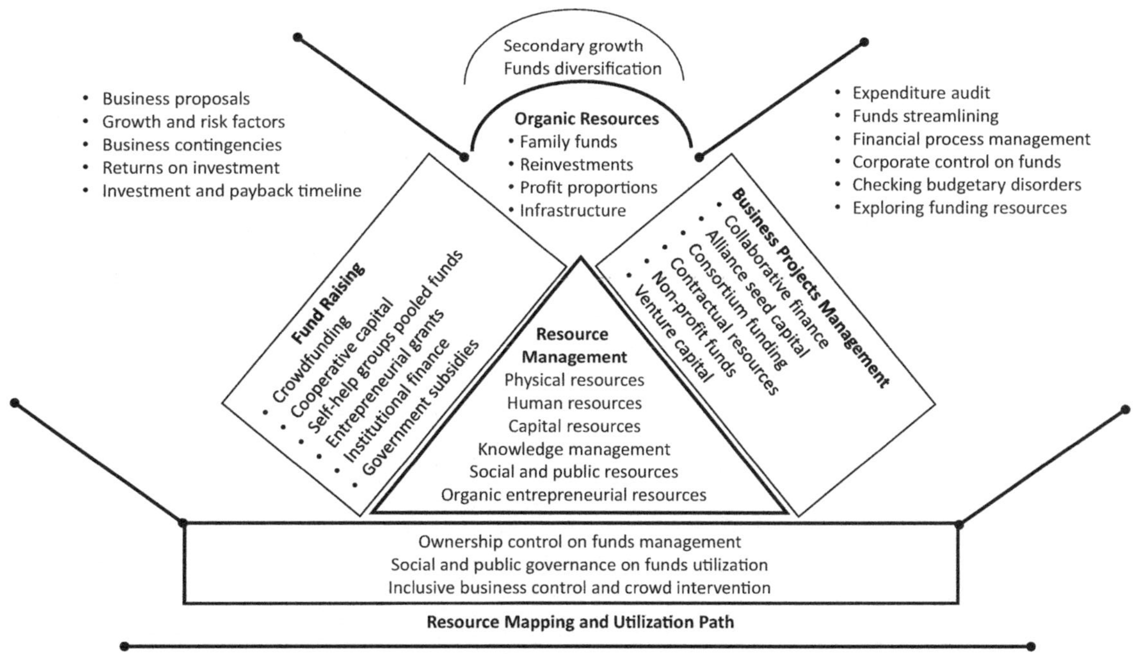

Fig. 4.2 Interdependencies across elements of financial resources in women enterprises (*Source* Author)

the entrepreneurs through innovative business proposals, which emphasize faster growth and lower risk within the given market ecosystem. The proposals describe the strategic timeline of returns on investment, and payback tenure of crowdfunded projects. Micro and small enterprises describe business contingencies in the context of low market receptivity, unsold inventories, and lower scale of business.

The principal intangible resource in micro and small enterprises is knowledge management, which is significantly related to the management of organic entrepreneurial resources emerging out of family businesses and creative social organizations. Knowledge management through continuous learning and experience sharing within society, peer entrepreneurs, and industry has become critical to achieving competitive advantages over technology adaptation, market-oriented designing, and the increasing market competitiveness. The increasing use of social media has leveraged collective intelligence, integrating market needs, and crowd emotions. Consequently, knowledge pooling and sharing have emerged as strategic tool to create value and increase effectiveness of operations management and entrepreneurial productivity. Knowledge management is also promoted within enterprises through employee engagement to use continuous learning systems and acquiring various knowledge portfolios (spatial and temporal dimensions of innovation, technology use, and marketing approaches) to improve organizational performance (Wang & Yang, 2016). Broadly, knowledge management is all about managing entrepreneurial knowledge in a systematic process within organizational ecosystem for acquiring, organizing, applying, and sharing tacit and explicit knowledge among employees. It is a continuous process often discontinued by micro and small entrepreneurs, as they focus on marketing and profiteering without enhancing the knowledge portfolios and their application in developing competitive products and following contemporary business practices (Dotsika & Patrick, 2013).

One of the progressive ways of streamlining financial requirements and utilization of funds is through developing collaborative business projects within the same entrepreneurial categories (size, type of production, target markets, and profitability) or with large companies. Such entrepreneurial collaboration ensures the availability of collaborative finance for administering fixed assets and working capital. The collaborators develop seed capital and encourage building contractual resources for mutual benefits by enhancing productivity, market competitiveness, and organizational performance. Agglomeration of micro and small enterprises engaged in identical business often form a consortium and raise activity-specific funds for carrying out low-cost innovation, pooled technology, customer-centric production, green packaging, and dynamic distribution. Commitment theory suggests that the strategic view on business operations improves the consortium performance (homogeneous alliances) to meet predetermined expectations. The continuity of consortium production in business operations leads to the enhancement of market opportunities and improvement of the extent of business partnering by reducing the potential risk and improving the scale of business, marketability, and profitability. Therefore, consortium resources (finance, human capital, raw material, and infrastructure) largely influence the business performance of alliance partners and minimize internal conflicts of organization. Such business project collaboration also has the potential to institute new trends in product consumptions, social values, and establishing high-end market leadership (Muthusamy & White, 2005). Collaborative business projects conduct periodical audits to streamline the flow of funds and check budgetary disorders. Supplementary funding is also explored collectively to support the need for additional investment for incremental production or business diversification (Lu et al., 2017).

Ownership control in managing funds among micro and small enterprises has been a major impediment in organizational performance. Ownership control has often emerged as the primary cause for misappropriation of entrepreneurial funds, affecting performance of enterprises. A contemporary solution of inclusive business by incorporating stakeholders (customers and investors) in resource control has proved to be successful in streamlining the resource utilization in various micro and small business firms. In addition, crowd intervention (crowdfunded projects), and social and public governance on utilization of funds have been instrumental in encouraging these firms to utilize funds by purpose and evaluate the performance of financial inputs on organizational output. Besides these financial governance measures, digitalization of financial flows in an organization has proved to be effective in establishing performance by objectives and control the resource drain within organization (Schilling & Werners, 2016).

Business Complexity Grid

Complexity has become the subdomain of management science, which affects various factors of business management from idea generation, decision-making, and exploiting business opportunities through individual or collective perspectives. Perceptions of leaders, employees, and stakeholders, which contribute to the business dynamics are often impaired in micro and small enterprises causing ideological drift and fragmentation in areas of decision. Commonly, the organizational complexity in single ownership firms is experienced to be lower than the partnership firms. Therefore, it appears appropriate to argue that one is company has monolithic business practices, two is company have fragmented decisions, and three is company appear to be a crowd. Complexity in business is blended with the personality traits of leaders and the nature of employees and stakeholders who are associated in decision-making and strategy implementation. Such organizational constitution looks like a crowd phenomenon, which encourages the tendency of ***participation first***, decisions based on contemporary trends, individual perceptions on challenges and opportunities, and individualistic appraisal of expected outcomes. These factors contribute to internal chaos in organization led by subjective interactions and objective interconnectedness across the emergent factors. The organizational complexities concerning business performance are often focused on the extent of profitability, innovation and technology, and market competitiveness. Such complexities overshadow the structured business operations and drive volatility in financial resources by multiple disjointed business perspectives and corresponding decisions. Consequently, the micro and small enterprises grow with unstable strategies of business operations, managing competition, and creating internal and external value chains. However, by deconstructing the entrepreneurial base with zero complexity bottom line, entrepreneurs can achieve breakthrough in business and reduce organizational resistance (Gottfredson & Aspinall, 2005).

Business complexities evolve around resource management in an enterprise. Financial management in emerging enterprises initially appears to be simple, but grows complex with diversification in the business portfolios, which causes cross-utilization of funds across portfolios and cannibalize financial resources. Other complexities like developing competitive business strategies, exploring new markets, creating design-centric (competition *vs* customers) culture, and deployment of employee autonomy in decision-making process are often detrimental to entrepreneurial growth. Therefore, managing entrepreneurial businesses irrespective of organizational size and market coverage requires the skills of gamesmanship to evaluate the situation, prepare the play, and plan for expected outcomes. Business complexities can be managed through cooperative competition, guerrilla strategy, and harvesting within minimum viable segments. To achieve these skills, entrepreneurs need to learn and employ *ombudsman strategy* to resolve the organizational issues through a single-window management system (MacMillan et al., 2003). Most micro and small enterprises emerge with innovative ideas, which are subjected to a robust experiment in the niche market or in exploring business links with alliance partners. Entrepreneurs architecting their firms with such ideas often fall into the amateur business trap and succumb to inordinate complications arising from resource drain, ineffective marketing, and myopic business performance. The experimental enterprises raise several questions on the purpose of business, stakeholder's commitment, sustainability of experiment, cause and effect relationship, blind tests and reliability of results, and concerns on managing value stream (Thomke & Manzi, 2014).

The use of contemporary technology, digitalization, and developing social media-based entrepreneurial performance appears to be simple in the initial stages of the business lifecycle but leads to complexities with the expansion of services, business portfolios, need for customization, and establishing virtual business securities. In this process, innovation and customer engagement help in embracing operational complexities and streamlining unreliability associated with various value chains (production, supply, and customer value). By involving market players and stakeholders in evaluating business experiments, entrepreneurs can seek appropriate solutions to overcome the triadic grid of complexities comprising people, performance, and profit (3Ps). Successful enterprises tend to differentiate their performance by deploying strategies to the front-line managers of the organization. Such practice helps entrepreneurs in overcoming the short- and long-run complexities (Allen & Zook, 2011). Among various types of complexities in business, organizational culture also contributes to chaos in managing business processes and achieving desired performance. Consequently, conventional wisdom driven by individualistic leadership causes several difficulties in transforming organizational skills, workplace flexibility, and employee engagement. These factors contribute to formidable advantages, which enable enterprises to outwit, outmaneuver, and outperform their competitors.

The extent of complexities in business can be reduced by using shared models of production, operations, accountability, and control within the organization. Nevertheless, managing with multiple shared functions is difficult, as they are often asynchronized and executed separately. The coordination among different functions helps organizations to develop a well-coordinated process map to reduce the complexities associated with cost, time, and risk (Casadesus-Masanell & Tarzijan, 2012).

Most micro and small enterprises develop business complexities with the escalation of cost and uncertainty in achieving the desired profit goals. Managing financial resources constitutes a major cause for inculcating process complications within production and business operations. The major challenge faced by these enterprises is toward the transformation of financial system comprising process transparency, cost reduction, yield optimization, and periodical performance audits. The complications in financial process tend to be more in shared accountability and control in the enterprises that are funded by external sources including corporate funding, crowdfunding, and institutional financing under government programs. Shared financial services focus on hierarchical accountability, unclear standards, and scattered performance projections across portfolios and time, which affects the organizational system related to strategic financial objectives, process designs, personnel system, and information coordination. Consequently, internal factors of the organization will restrain the competitive advantage of the enterprise due to shared financial operations and controls (Duysters & Lokshin, 2011). Knowledge management is considered to be a critical resource for the development of competitive advantage by minimizing the internal complexities within a business organization. Shifts in knowledge-management culture often disturb the workplace culture due to social and innate resistance toward reorienting the production and business operation system. Such asymmetrical behavior among the employees of the organization often contributes to internal chaos by damaging the trust and willingness to change in the new knowledge-friendly organizational culture. Consequently, the workplace complexities affect competitive advantage and organizational performance of firms. The complexity in workplace culture is often triggered by the organizational policies on knowledge sharing, co-creation, shared accountability, and shared performance measurements (Intezari et al., 2017). The intricacy in entrepreneurial business is largely observed in various chaotic situations across employees, stakeholders, and leaders of the firm. These attributes are categorically exhibited in Fig. 4.3.

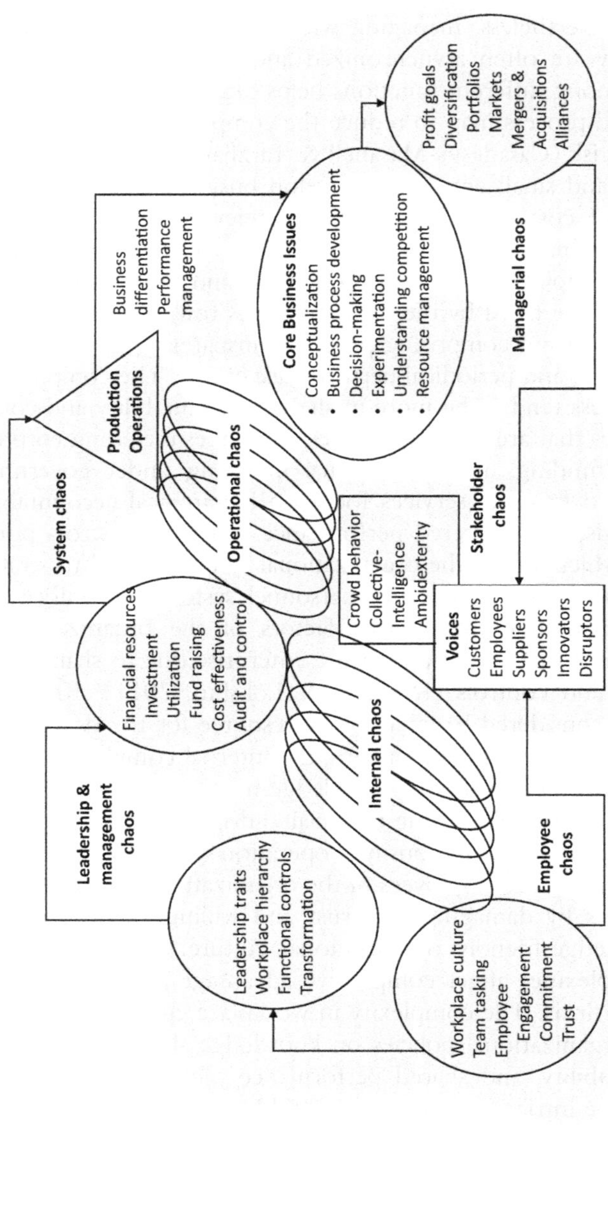

Fig. 4.3 Intricacies in entrepreneurial business (*Source* Author)

The core business issues in micro and small enterprises are spread across multiple dimensions beginning with the conceptualization of business (idea generation and idea confirmation), development of business process specific to business concepts and markets, and making appropriate decisions to uphold the business ideas and operational plans. As these enterprises are weak in defining business concepts, entrepreneurs often tend to experiment with business ideas, innovation, and marketing strategies without a thorough understanding of market competition and embedded impediments. Consequently, micro and small enterprises face critical issues in managing entrepreneurial resources, which include raw material, finance, human capital, and infrastructure associated with production and operations. It has been argued in previous studies that these enterprises are not built on precise objectives, which causes operational inefficiency and lack of integrity in process improvement and changes management. Therefore, these firms are unable to develop conflict resolution protocols and involve entrepreneurial leaders to guide the business in complex situations. The internal incompetence and confusion make these firms employ external consultants to guarantee the streamlining of the business process, implementation, and setting up accountability (Klein, 2017).

Business complexities in micro and small enterprises lead to both internal and operational chaos. The leadership attributes (individualistic and autocratic) largely influence the internal complexities as they tend to monitor and control internal business processes and establish workplace hierarchy. The internal business process is affected by the decision-making behavior of entrepreneurial leaders while setting up functional controls and initiating the transformational process. Therefore, there are possibilities of triggering internal chaos during the implementation of change management policies. In addition, the conventional workplace culture comprising multi-tasking and multiple reporting also affects the organizational culture and workplace dynamics. These factors affect employee engagement, commitment, and trust within the organization (Smith et al., 2019). Employee engagement and flexible workplace practices help in reducing internal chaos caused by decision delays, insufficient evidence-based decisions, and lack of transparency in communication. These factors combined contribute to reducing the overall management chaos and leadership complexities, which leads to controlling the complexities in resource management, and production and operations management. However, despite the popular appeal of workplace flexibility and collective leadership, the adaptation to these practices is relatively low, as managers convey disapproval to the collective processes because of the feeling of not leveraging the authoritative control (Williams et al., 2013).

The unclear policies in managing financial resources (as family businesses practice conventional controls on finance), investments, and utilization of funds in production, operations, and administrative overheads often intricate entrepreneurial and business operations. The concept of fundraising is not fully evolved in micro and small enterprises, though these firms are aware of various sources of fundraising such as crowdfunding, corporate and international grants, and institutional funds. Consequently, these enterprises fail to attract adequate external funds and manage them cost-effectively. In addition, small enterprises face various constraints in obtaining finances to support their production and business operations due to rigid regulations, tax structure, and lack of managerial know-how. These factors lead to financial chaos, and the firms have to compromise to run their business operations with deficient capital, high operating costs, and incapability to obtain market borrowings; and they fail in meeting financial requirements to ensure their firms and protecting revenue from losses (Lownes-Jackson et al., 2003). Most micro and small enterprises face challenges in improving their financial literacy to improve the managerial know-how toward understanding and analyzing financial standards, data, and temporal and spatial trends of financial ratios. Thus, the entrepreneurial leaders; who often hold combined portfolios of chief executive officer, chief operating officer, and chief financial officer in their firms; fail to take appropriate financial decisions due to biased judgements (Lusardi & Mitchell, 2014). The internal chaos ultimately thrusts complexities in productions and operations management causing internal systems chaos in organizations.

Complexity in organizations is also driven by the stakeholders comprising customers and investors who stay demanding to gain competitive advantage at par with the industry. The crowd behavior and collective intelligence also contribute to new perspectives among customers, which often creates uncertainty within the firm in meeting the radical (self-concepts) and learned (collective intelligence) preferences. In enterprises with democratic organizational culture, the voices of employees and customers are critical in making managerial decisions and implementing inclusive business perspectives to deliver desired values. The micro and small enterprises seeking external sponsorship (donations, grants, and seed capital) often yield to the sponsor's voice in developing policies on productions and operations management. In addition, innovators developing prototypes for entrepreneurial firms also raise voice for, and against, entrepreneurial policies and seek co-creation of strategies on production and business operations. However, technological, production, and service disruptions often create chaos in the external ecosystem of enterprises, which drives instability in decision-making and portraying future projections on business performance.

References

Adams, D., Adams, K., Ullah, S., & Ullah, F. (2019, June). Globalisation, governance, accountability and the natural resource 'curse': Implications for socio-economic growth of oil-rich developing countries. *Resources Policy, 61*, 128–140.

Allen, J., & Zook, C. (2011). The great repeatable business model. *Harvard Business Review, 89*(11)

Avadhanam, R., & Pidikiti, J. (2014). *ALEAP: A leap of faith for women entrepreneurs*. Harvard Business School Press.

Casadesus-Masanell, R., & Ricart, J. E. (2011). How to design a winning business model. *Harvard Business Review.*

Casadesus-Masanell, R., & Tarzijan, J. (2012). When one business model isn't enough? *Harvard Business Review, 90*(1–2), 1–5.

Chang, Y. Y., & Chen, M. H. (2020). Creative entrepreneurs' creativity, opportunity recognition, and career success: Is resource availability a double-edged sword? *European Management Journal, 38*(5), 750–762.

Christensen, C. M., Bartman, T., & van Bever, D. C. M. (2016). The hard truth about business model innovation. *MIT Sloan Management Review, 58*(1), 31–40.

Christensen, C. M., & Overdorf, M. (2000). Meeting the challenge of disruptive change. *Harvard Business Review, 78*(2), 67–76.

Chemmanur, J. T., Karthik, K., & Debarshi, K. N. (2011). How does venture capital financing improve efficiency in private firms? A look beneath the surface. *Review of Financial Studies, 24*(12), 4037–4090.

Cooper, R., & Slagmulder, R. (2004). Achieving full-cycle cost management. *MIT Sloan Management Review, 46*(1), 45–52.

Davenport, T. H., Harris, J., & Shapiro, J. (2010). Competing on talent analytics. *Harvard Business Review, 88*(10), 52–58.

Dotsika, F., & Patrick, K. (2013). Collaborative KM for SMEs: A framework evaluation study. *Information Technology & People, 26*(4), 368–382.

Duysters, G., & Lokshin, B. (2011). Determinants of alliance portfolio complexity and its effect on innovative performance of companies. *Journal of Product Innovation Management, 28*(4), 570–585.

Dyer, J. H., Kale, P., Singh, H., & Singh, H. (2001). How to make strategic alliances work. *MIT Sloan Management Review, 42*(4), 37–43.

Eller, R., Alford, P., Kallmünzer, A., & Peters, M. (2020). Antecedents, consequences, and challenges of small and medium-sized enterprise digitalization. *Journal of Business Research, 112*(5), 119–127.

Gottfredson, M., & Aspinall, K. (2005). Innovation versus complexity: What is too much of a good thing? *Harvard Business Review, 83*(11), 62–71.

Gottfredson, M., Puryear, R., & Phillips, S. (2005). Strategic sourcing: From periphery to the core. *Harvard Business Review, 83*(2), 132–139.

Gulati, R., Sytch, M., & Mehrotra, P. (2008). Breaking up is never easy: Planning for exit in a strategic alliance. *California Management Review, 50*(4), 147–163.

Holt, D. B. (2016). Branding in the age of social media. *Harvard Business Review, 94*(3), 40–48.

Iansiti, M., & Lakhani, K. R. (2014). Digital ubiquity: How connections, sensors, and data are revolutionizing business. *Harvard Business Review, 92*(11), 1–7.

Ibarra, H., & Hansen, M. T. (2011). Are you a collaborative leader? *Harvard Business Review, 89*(7–8), 68–74.

Intezari, A., Taskin, N., & Pauleen, D. J. (2017). Looking beyond knowledge sharing: An integrative approach to knowledge management culture. *Journal of Knowledge Management, 21*(2), 492–515.

Klein, T. (2017). *Why are startup founders so bad at changing their own companies?* Harvard Business School Publication.

Lee, I. H., Kim, S. M., & Green, s. (2021). Social enterprises and market performance: The moderating roles of innovativeness, sectoral alignment, and geographic localization. *Journal of Business Research, 132*, 491–506.

Liu, Y., Combs, J. G., Ketchen, D. J., & Ireland, R. D. (2007). The value of human resource management for organizational performance. *Business Horizons, 50*(6), 503–511.

Lownes-Jackson, M., Olorunniwo, F., Flott, P., & Ellzy, J. (2003). Financial obstacles faced by African American entrepreneurs: An insight into a developing area of the US economy. *The Journal of Developing Areas, 36*(2), 125–145.

Lu, P., Yuan, S., & Wu, J. (2017). The interaction effect between intra-organizational and inter-organizational control on the project performance of new product development in open innovation. *International Journal of Project Management, 35*(8), 1627–1638.

Lusardi, A., & Mitchell, O. S. (2014). The economic importance of financial literacy: Theory and evidence. *Journal of Economic Literature, 52*(1), 5–44.

MacMillan, I. C., Van Putten, A. B., & McGrath, R. G. (2003). Global gamesmanship. *Harvard Business Review, 81*(5), 62–71.

Mathwick, C. (2017). *Business model innovation at Wildfang*. North American Case Research Association (NACRA), 1–12.

McDonald, R., & Eisenhardt, K. M. (2020). The new-market conundrum. *Harvard Business Review* (Digital Article).

Muthusamy, S., & White, M. (2005). Learning and knowledge transfer in strategic alliances: A social exchange. *Organization Studies, 26*(3), 415–441.

Nidumolu, R., Prahalad, C. K., & Rangaswami, M. R. (2009). Why sustainability is now the key driver of innovation. *Harvard Business Review, 41*(2), 30–37.

Ovans, A. (2015). What is a business model? *Harvard Business Review* (Digital article). https://hbr.org/2015/01/what-is-a-business-model

Porter, M. E., & Heppelmann, J. (2014). How smart, connected products are transforming competition. *Harvard Business Review, 92*(1), 1–18.

Rajagopal. (2021). *The business design cube: Converging markets, society, and customer values to grow competitive in business*. Business Expert Press.

Rajagopal, Solano, R., Burgos, F., & Gamboa, L. (2013). The spirit behind Talavera de la Reyna: Angelca Moreno's pottery. In M. F. Guillen (Ed.), *Women entrepreneurs: Inspiring stories from emerging economies and developing countries*. Routledge.

Schilling, A., & Werners, B. (2016). Optimal selection of IT security safeguards from an existing knowledge base. *European Journal of Operational Research, 248*(1), 318–327.

Smith, E. F., Gilmer, D. O., & Stockdale, M. S. (2019). The importance of culture and support for workplace flexibility: An ecological framework for understanding flexibility support structures. *Business Horizons, 62*(5), 557–566.

Sutton, R. I. (2001). Weird rules of creativity. *Harvard Business Review, 79*(8), 94–103.

Thomke, S., & Manzi, J. (2014). The discipline of business experimentation. *Harvard Business Review, 92*(12), 1–10.

Todeschini, B. V., Cortimiglia, M. N., Callegaro-de-Menezes, D., & Ghezzi, A. (2017). Innovative and sustainable business models in the fashion industry: Entrepreneurial drivers, opportunities, and challenges. *Business Horizons, 60*(6), 759–770.

Tóth, Z., Nieroda, M. E., & Koles, B. (2020). Becoming a more attractive supplier by managing references—The case of small and medium-sized enterprises in a digitally enhanced business environment. *Industrial Marketing Management, 84*, 312–327.

Wang, M. H., & Yang, T. Y. (2016). Investigating the success of knowledge management: An empirical study of small- and medium-sized enterprises. *Asia Pacific Management Review, 21*(2), 79–91.

Weill, P., & Woerner, S. (2015). Thriving in an increasingly digital ecosystem. *MIT Sloan Management Review, 56*(4), 27–34.

Welsh, J. A. & White, J. F. (1981). Small business is not a little big business. *Harvard Business Review*, 1–11.

Williams, J. C., Blair-Loy, M., & Berdahl, J. L. (2013). Cultural schemas, social class, and the flexibility stigma. *Journal of Social Issues, 69*(2), 209–234.

Wong, M. (2019). *Helarctos ventures: Investing in seed-stage start-ups*. Harvard Business School Press.

CHAPTER 5

Gender, Innovations, and Ecosystems

Abstract This chapter presents an array of discussions on innovation management in low-cost social enterprises to attract market competitiveness, societal values, and creativity booms (Crittenden, V. L., Crittenden, W. F., & Ajjan, H. (2019). Empowering women micro-entrepreneurs in emerging economies: The role of information communications technology. *Journal of Business Research, 98*, 191–203). In addition, entrepreneurial ecosystems constitute the core discussion in this chapter. The general discussion on innovation and ecosystems in the context of gender-sensitive entrepreneurship has been presented in reference to the role of women in social and business enterprises within the broad global framework.

Keywords Society and creativity · Gender · Ecosystem · Innovation management · Collective intelligence · Market competitiveness · Challenges and prospects

The role of women in society has been a matter of debate over the past. The social and economic rights of women and their empowerment in society have evolved with several social movements and shifts in sociopolitical ideologies over the twentieth century, which have encouraged women entrepreneurs to perform in business with gender

A. Rajagopal, *Women Entrepreneurs in Emerging Markets*, International Marketing and Management Research,
https://doi.org/10.1007/978-3-030-89770-3_5

equality. However, the chronological evolution of concepts related to gender equality, equity, and economic empowerment has become a regional discourse though there is international concern on the social and economic rights of women. Therefore, the discussion on feminism embedded in international forums is radically different from the concern on the excellence of women in business and society. In the context of modern sociopolitical philosophy, feminism has emerged as a critical change to social orthodoxy and primitive entrepreneurial democratism. The classical thinkers Thomas Hobbes, John Locke, and Jean-Jacques Rousseau, who have contributed to the social contract theory, emphasize that women in society also significantly support the family habits and lifestyles, which are the outgrowths of social and economic forces. They also mentioned that the equality among males was based on their actual and derived advantage over women in the society. Consequently, masculinity in the society has grown as a prominent factor of governance within family and society at large (Valcárcel, 2002).

In the contemporary global environment, the participation of women continues to grow but the gender performance gap could not be eliminated completely. There are various internal (family, personality, and culture) and external forces (Social acceptance, economic opportunities, and public policies) that affect the differential inputs and value perspectives by gender. These factors explain the criticality of gender performance gap by emphasizing the cognitive ergonomics among women, social identity, economic equality, and public support. Entrepreneurship in society has cultivated masculine emotions in business with the notion of power, patronage, and performance in entrepreneurial ventures. Consequently, the psycho-sociological effects on women entrepreneurs have diminished their capabilities and competencies to serve as real entrepreneurs or exhibit success at par with masculine standards (Ladge et al., 2019). Sociopolitical shifts in manifesting minority entrepreneurship have reconceptualized empowerment of women who constituted an economic minority in conventional societies and engrossed the liberty of women. Consequently, feminism has reemerged in developing economies with the support of social leadership and public policies, which have motivated women to establish entrepreneurial activities and enter with equality in conducting business across the social boundaries. The mainstream business agglomeration and media organizations have encouraged women entrepreneurs to accept business leaderships by representing gender appropriately within the industry and community. Accordingly, feminism has supported women to overcome gender issues concerning business leadership, creativity and manufacturing, and marketing of products and services within the social and business taxonomy (Schiele et al., 2020). Such change in entrepreneurial philosophy has motivated women to develop their own brands. Over time, many female-owned fashion brands have emerged globally by strengthening the gender concerns and the contest for economic equity among women. One of the examples of prominent female-led brands within the women-centric fashion industry is Susan Alexandra, a brand after the name of the female entrepreneur that has been regarded for the 3C attributes comprising creativity, collective intelligence, and conscious consumerism.

Liberal feminism has propagated in developed countries, and big emerging markets demonstrate the fundamental rights of men and women in pursuing economic activities and conceptualize that both genders are the same in managing entrepreneurial ventures. However, the gender concerns stemming out of the conventional ideologies differ from ubiquitous perspectives on women's liberation for economic freedom and for developing the desired values and lifestyle within society. Such movement unveils economic opportunities for women and encourages them to demonstrate their abilities out of the box through entrepreneurship, voice, and experience. These factors bring fundamental differences across the genders and help women in overcoming the social inferiority and dominant patriarchy within the family ecosystem (Hearn & Hein, 2015). Therefore, feminism today has evolved as a multifaceted movement, which integrates modern (social and economic liberty) and hybrid (social media, digital enterprises, and augmented reality) feminist themes. Media has been the key influencer of women's economic rights in the twenty-first century, which has altered precarious meanings, social relations, and economic representations of women. Such socioeconomic shift in gender sensitization has provided robust propositions on capability, competency, and leadership attributes of women (England et al., 2011). The Gender Schema Theory illustrates new cognitive structures supported by collective intelligence and the role of media, which demonstrates the influence of new economic opportunities across genders for integrated economic growth and social development. This theory discusses various economic ecosystems, which empowers women entrepreneurs and recognizes the purchasing power of young female consumers, which builds mutual support in the business. The consumers have also developed new cognitive frameworks infused by media on *girl power* and *pro-girl* concepts to develop interdependency and collinearity between women entrepreneurs, female entrepreneurial brands, and feminine thematic products. Such behavior has inculcated positive changes in support of the contemporary feminist philosophy and role of women entrepreneurs in changing business environments (Murray et al., 2019).

Society and Creativity

Social enterprises are tagged with creativity to enhance social values within the community and grow within the niche unlike commercial enterprises expanding their business with a market-oriented approach. Therefore, it is evident from previous literature that society and creativity are highly correlated and help enterprises in developing more social products than commercial products. However, the economic perspective of creativity in society emphasizes innovation, value, and economic benefits embedded in social enterprises that are transforming with commercial business models. Women entrepreneurs are the edge of social enterprises, who are encouraged in liberal economies to converge social and business enterprises for mutual growth by anchoring creativity, social values, and consumer consciousness. Society and creativity are linked with the design thinking perspectives that stimulate ideation, innovation, and propagation within the society and consumer segments. The design thinking (Liedtka, 2018) embedded in emerging social and commercial enterprises at the grassroots of the society helps investors and customers, who constitute a broader group of stakeholders, to overcome the problems associated with 4As (Awareness, Availability, Affordability, and Adaptability). The design thinking provides an opportunity to stakeholders and users to unveil creative ideation based on perceptions, knowledge, and experience. The market research exploring the contemporary trends congruent with the design thinking would help in developing successful entrepreneurial business models to experiment with new solutions. Such a process requires entrepreneurs to develop a clear structure in the context of idea generation, conceptualization, concept testing, market testing, and pre-commercialization business strategies development. The design thinking is convergent with the divergent factors of design-to-market, design-to-society, and design-to-value (Rajagopal, 2021a).

Progressive societies with liberal thinking, gender equality, and equity of women entrepreneurs could be the appropriate platform for cultivating creativity and innovative products through mass collaborations.

Brainstorming the unfinished ideas across social platforms including face-to-face and digital networks enhances cooperation and productivity in transforming the creative prototypes of entrepreneurs into commercial products. Therefore, the social capital contributes significantly in transforming entrepreneurial products into commercial products and in developing significant social value by generating a high ethnic, environmental, and emotional composite index (3E composite index). However, commercialization of innovations evolved on social foundations faces several challenges including the off-trend concepts, focus on commercialization, and in-depth customer centricity. Consequently, innovations with diversity and considerable openness often succumb to the lack of cohesiveness between the conceptualizing innovation and its commercialization strategies (Florida et al., 2002). Public policies, collective intelligence, and corporate social responsibility have infused the sense of commercialization and business dynamics in the micro and small enterprises as a principal economic stimulus. The conceptualization of innovative ideas at micro enterprises emerges out of an unconventional business plan, which is supported by the public policies at large, and the commercial segment to some extent, to transform innovations within the market ecosystem. The low-end marketing strategies strengthen the niche market and the initial layers of competitive markets, while the upstream markets grow with the corporate sponsorship of selected innovative products developed at the grassroots (Montgomery, 2008).

The entrepreneurial mindfulness influences business thinking in varied social ambiences ranging from conservative economics to positive entrepreneurial psychology. Successful women enterprises at the bottom-of-the-pyramid and in upstream markets evolve around socioeconomic values, ethnic features and collective abilities, which tend to auto pilot the innovations in niche markets. Such efforts involve high risk, high stress, and low economic gains during the initial phase of business transformation, and unlock creativity for wider marketing performance. Consequently, the microenterprises in their initial stages cocoon their growth in niche markets and look for a corporate business lift to take advantage of new opportunities and grow as inclusive business firms. Microfinance companies, which have grown as banking institutions over a period, have evolved on social platforms with the support of public policies, and corporate financial alliances have grown as larger business entities (Langer & Beard, 2014). Inclusive businesses in Asia and Latin American regions are growing as commercial businesses upscaling innovative and systematic solutions to the problems of bottom-of-the-pyramid consumer segments. Such companies largely establish value chains to bring positive changes among women's lives and tend to reduce gender inequality by maximizing financial returns and social impact. The commercially viable innovations, which are transformed into viable business models, considerably support the women's economic advancement in the areas of agribusiness, health, education, energy, financial services, manufacturing, urban facilities, information and communication technology, and retail business segments. The inclusivity in business helps in increasing employment, productivity, income, and the related products improving quality of life. Consequently, inclusive enterprises empower women enterprises by breaking the complexity of social process and establishing economic leverage through gender inclusiveness (Asian Development Bank, 2016).

Digital transformation in entrepreneurship has encouraged social creativity as a continuous process through digital interactions among entrepreneurs, stakeholders, and customers. Consequently, the collective intelligence has emerged as a mainstream ideation process in start-up enterprises, which is largely based on the consumer cognition, value perspectives, and customer-centricity philosophy embedded in enterprises to gain market competitiveness. In addition, social creative thinkers illustrate their ideas for catering to a community cause such as sustainability-based business, innovation in social health products, developing innovative educational tools, sustainable housing, and the like (Luqman et al., 2021). Convergence of consumers, stakeholders, and creative commons acts as the entrepreneurial bridge to outreach competitive markets and the *big-middle* (triadic growth of upper, regular, and lower mass consumer segments). Most start-up enterprises led by women entrepreneurs are based on creativity as a driving tool of innovation overcoming the stereotyped competition of utilitarian and hedonic products. These enterprises often go to crowds to generate, endorse, and transform (GET) ideas as the creative capital to stand out in the radical competition and evolve into a unique entrepreneurial posture. Therefore, the GET philosophy has emerged as a new tool to generate ideas and communication, and develop bottom-up business models for achieving success in niche markets (Rajagopal, 2021b). Developing creative capital is a major challenge for emerging enterprises, as they need to effectively harness the creative inputs and energize the commercialization of innovation by integrating the coordinated efforts of stakeholders, customers, technology developers, entrepreneurial leaders, managers, and employees. The entrepreneurial leaders are responsible for triggering collective creativity and driving social communities to participate in the creativity process. It is necessary for the leaders to eliminate competitive distractions and arbitrary preferences of consumers, which restrict the transformation of collective ideas to commercial business models. Therefore, engaging customers in creativity process embeds emotions, personality, perceived use value, and conscious consumption behavior in the process of creativity and commercialization of new business ideas such as production and operations (Florida & Goodnight, 2005).

The critical path to commercialization of innovation passes through society and creativity as exhibited in Fig. 5.1. This is an upstream innovation from niche market to competitive business environment, which is driven by crowd behavior, social cognition, and consumer consciousness. Consequently, the creative nexus, which embeds the creative continuum, involves consumer cognition and participatory business appraisal demonstrated jointly by society, customers, and stakeholders. The social domain of supporting creative innovations has several drivers comprising social awareness, social problems, social needs, social initiatives, and community leadership, which stimulate creativity among social entrepreneurs. The contemporary perspectives on creative entrepreneurship advocate gender equality and implementing inclusive business model by involving customers and stakeholders as business associates. In addition, the contemporary perspectives also emphasize the 3E factors comprising ethnic, environmental, and emotional attributes contributing to the process of commercialization of innovation. The involvement of society in nurturing creative enterprises needs consistent social governance to manage creative capital, reverse accountability (customers and stakeholders voice in decision-making), and community involvement in determining the commercialization perspectives of innovations. In addition, the GET philosophy emphasizes generating, endorsing, and transforming the generic and collective ideas with appropriate marketing and communication mix to gain competitive leverage on innovative products and services.

Creativity in nascent enterprises is affected by consumer choices and crowd behavior leading to creative commons. This process leads to the accumulation of innovative ideas, prototypes, and pilot test results of the low-cost innovation and technology embedded with customer value. However, commercialization of creative business ideas and innovations faces a major challenge for emerging women-led enterprises as it requires

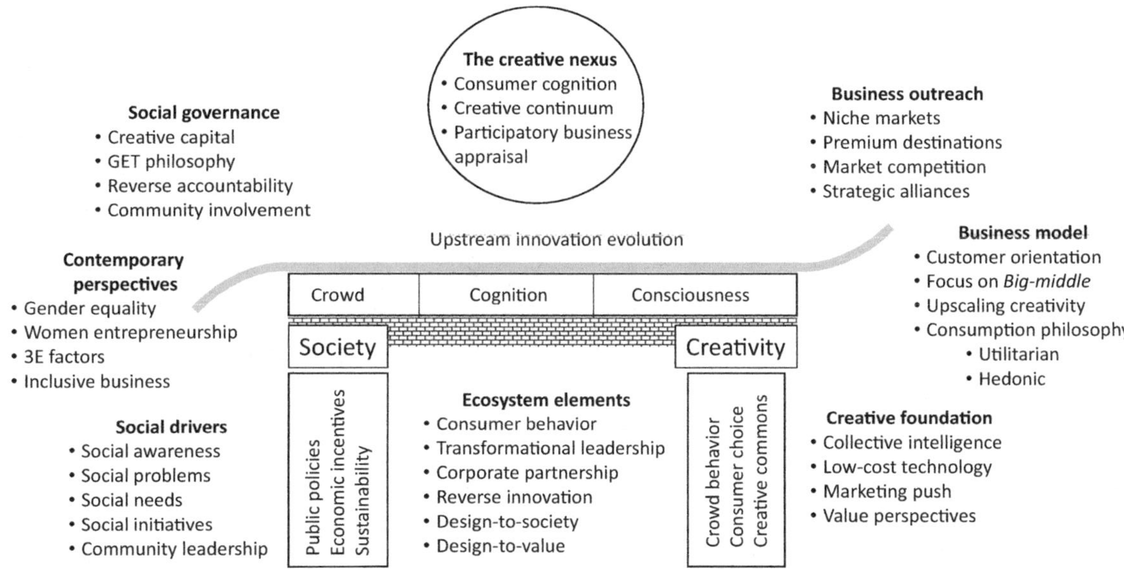

Fig. 5.1 Society and creativity path to commercialization (*Source* Author)

competitive marketing push involving moderate to high investment. Some enterprises have been benefitted from the crowdsourcing and crowd-funding strategies, which support them in improving the capital resources needed for marketing push. The lessons learned from collective intelligence and crowd behavior have directed many enterprises to establish customer orientation in commercializing their innovation and focus on the *big-middle* consumer segment. These strategies help in upscaling creativity to cater to utilitarian and hedonic perspectives of consumption behavior, and enhance the business outreach from niche markets to premium markets overriding the market competition to some extent. The strategic alliances of micro and small enterprises with large companies facilitate the evolution of innovation to upstream markets. The convergence of society and creativity in commercializing the innovations needs effective transformational leadership and corporate partnership. The design-to-society and design-to-value concepts help in developing pro-enterprise consumer behavior.

Most women entrepreneurs operate on an experiential spectrum introspecting their capabilities and competence, and societal endorsements on their entrepreneurial abilities. Accordingly, women entrepreneurs nurture creativity in their enterprises on a mixed business philosophy supported by the social values, personal growth, and entrepreneurial profit. Consequently, women-led enterprises are based on double bottom lines comprising personal growth and the commercialization of entrepreneurial ideas. In this process, women entrepreneurs seek support from family, society, and fraternity. The collective intelligence plays a significant role in idea generation, implementation, and continuous learning with incremental innovations among the women enterprise. In addition, public policies, and interactions with the stakeholder support women entrepreneurs in recognizing the challenges and developing business models from the point of view of profit-with-purpose. This is the distant form of evolution of women enterprises by maximizing social values and return on investment with conscious engagement in managing entrepreneurial creativity. Most women entrepreneurs require cradle-to-cradle support in managing enterprises, which are emerging out of family business and targeting to grow as lead commercial ventures. The above managerial attributes are embedded with the LIFE paradigm, which advocates social and economic liberty, converging individual and collective intelligence, networking with peers (fraternity), and demanding social and economic equity (Saebi et al., 2019).

Innovation Management

The journey of innovation in micro and small enterprises begin with amateur ideation in the inner entrepreneurial circle comprising leaders and employees. However, the broad scope of innovations is explored and defined in the outer entrepreneurial circle including customers, stakeholders, and crowd at large. In developing innovations, the major challenge is hidden in exploring the consumer needs, perceived value, and the consumption philosophy covering the utilitarian and hedonic aspects. Market exploitability is also a demanding proposition in developing and managing innovations. Consequently, the end point of the journey of innovation is commercialization by ensuring the social and personal values of end users. The collective intelligence has emerged as a boon for innovators of micro and small enterprises who get a plethora of customer-centric and business-to-business ideas queuing for manufacturing and marketing within the competitive market ecosystem. Most entrepreneurs use digital technology tools and processes, and redefine their organizational structures to proactively lead innovations with varied disruptive attributes. Such innovation ecosystem not only provides the competitive advantage, but also help in developing customer orientation to unfamiliar brands and low-cost innovations based on homegrown technologies. For micro and small enterprises, building successful innovation journey requires customer-centricity, experiential marketing approaches, and contextual innovations to engage customers in cocreation and consumption process, and foster repeat buying behavior among consumers for low-cost innovations. Therefore, it is necessary to deploy the concept of an innovation journey manager in micro and small enterprises to monitor the evolution of innovation across predefined stages (Edelman & Singer, 2015).

Innovation in micro and small enterprises evolves as a single destination experiment with limited capital and human resources. These innovation experiments are largely longitudinal, which are backed by incremental innovations subject to their availability of resources and infrastructure. The single destination projects evolve within the niche market and grow with implicit knowledge and trust among stakeholders, customers, and employees. The entrepreneurial leadership also plays a significant role in driving cognitive dynamics among the human capital of the enterprise and evolves as a team contribution by sharing experience, culture, functional agility, and shared learning as the project unfolds. Most importantly, the innovation emerges as a small informal ideation seed, which is supported by the experiential knowledge, technical capabilities, and consumer perceptions as the innovation process continues. Starting small with innovations encompasses initial complexities of decision-making and experimental analytics. One of the many challenges at this stage is the continuous interactions with stakeholders, customers, and employees, and channelizing communication properly to build knowledge repositories.

Collective intelligence supports knowledge repositories to refine innovations, develop trust in ideas, and demonstrate competencies to plan their effective commercial execution. In the organizational context, innovation-led ideas often develop initial dichotomy in proposing innovative business models. Such rift in the organizations commonly occurs in accepting the change management process to accommodate innovation, business models, and associated risks. Consequently, micro and small enterprises need restructuring of organization by encouraging teamworking models and transformative leadership in lieu of nurturing innovations with conventional wisdom. With the advancement of innovations, changing the organizational design to integrate multi-disciplinary functions becomes an uphill task. The critical decisions are often deferred in these enterprises due to limited human capital, organizational capabilities, and competencies. Therefore, managing the innovation requires skilled talents with effective management focus and leadership drive. The ambiance for innovation in micro and small enterprises needs to be developed in the context of multi-disciplinary workstations to encourage research and development and exploit the global talent through alliances and digital networks.

Managing innovations in micro and small enterprises is largely centralized and driven by the entrepreneurial leaders, which limits the individual creativity and sense of organizational belongingness among employees. Consequently, the individual initiatives are oppressed and affect crucial decisions in carrying out the innovations across the different stages of the project. Such organizational problems cause deformity in communications, individual initiatives, and teamwork philosophy. These problems further attribute to the risk factors in managing innovations due to operational dilemmas and administrative complexities. To overcome these nascent problems, innovation in micro and small enterprises needs to be considered as a project instead of a single organizational task. Innovation projects need to be coordinated by an efficient project manager who assumes the charge of developing the complete project charter, sets stage-gate process, takes approval of toll gates periodically to conform with the project continuum, and avoid the project scope-creep (entertaining unplanned project deviations causing the effects of cost-time-risk). A too early announcement of innovation outcome might attract market disruptors causing the outgrowth of competitive products to cannibalize the expected innovation. Contrary to this, the delayed announcement of innovation outcome limits consumers in acquiring required information about the attributes and making appropriate buying decisions. Consequently, micro and small enterprises might use the social media channels to diffuse innovation outcomes within time limits. The communication and innovation should embed ethnic, cultural, and value-oriented information to facilitate the consumer knowledge. All innovations should be supported by effective service architecture to add value to the decision-making of consumers toward adapting to innovations.

One of the fundamental requirements for seeding and nurturing innovations in micro and small enterprises is toward managing financial and human resources, their allocation in carrying specific tasks, and investing in building capability and competence of employees. In developing economies, women-led enterprises are largely supported through various public policies in augmenting financial resources to be conditionally used in developing innovation and technology-based projects. The self-help groups, consortium enterprises, cooperatives, and corporate-sponsored women-led enterprises mediate resource planning with their partner organizations and monitor its implementation through social governance or reverse accountability (Wilson & Doz, 2012). In the digital economy, ecosystem-intelligent enterprises tend to collaborate with competent firms in the technology markets to gain market competitiveness in divergent consumer segments. Enterprises enhance their knowledge base and operate in specialized sectors using interactive platforms, and manage knowledge collectively. These firms cooperate with their business partners, customers, and stakeholders to collaborate, create, and communicate (3C's) knowledge with customers and market players to diffuse, distinguish, and deliver (3D's) innovations. The functionality of micro and small enterprises with 3C's and 3D's innovation management concept, break hierarchical governance mechanism of the conventional organizational design. Such transformation integrates the 3C's and 3D's concepts. These enterprises lead to distributed innovation, which capitalizes on the creativity of its collaborators, customers, and stakeholders to gain market competitiveness.

Distributive innovation is a refined version of collaborative innovation in which the micro and small enterprises tend to break the chaos of disruptive innovations and channelize innovations-to-market (Jarvenpaa & Välikangas, 2014). The distributed innovation management also has a concept identical to umbrella creation (community creation), which is largely emphasized as open innovation and linked to open market-based innovation model. In managing community creativity, the social firms act as sponsors and define the ground rules for active market players including customers, stakeholders, and partner firms. This is a blended innovation management model that integrates hierarchical management and an open market system. However, there is a risk of shifts and consumer preferences, penetration of disruptive innovations, and unpredicted market chaos in this model. Therefore, firms need to be more attentive to the market shifts in managing umbrella creation models, and more proactive to competitive knowledge and skills in managing innovations. The market ecosystem today has grown dynamic, flexible, assorted, and cohesive. These attributes demand creation of collaborative knowledge along with the entire innovation and marketing teams to stay dominant in a given market at a given time (Boland & Tenkasi, 1995). The attributes of innovation management process are illustrated in Fig. 5.2.

In the increasing competition and disruption in the business process caused by the changing attractiveness in industries, the competitive architecture of innovation management has become inevitable irrespective of the size of the enterprise. Figure 5.2 exhibits the innovation management architecture and its moderation across different players in commercializing innovations. The business entities engaged in architecting innovation management encompass innovators, suppliers, and vendors at the grassroot levels while the users, referrals, collaborators, and sponsors moderate the upscaling of innovation projects. In addition, public policies, community, and social leaders serve as drivers in managing innovations effectively. Therefore, the players in innovation management, as discussed above, constitute the ground stage of innovation management process. The foreground of innovation management process has seven stages comprising ideation, concept development, concept testing, market testing, market planning, business functions, and commercialization of innovation. Entrepreneurs tend to explore ideation for innovations within the organization by observing market trends, acting on social stimulus, learning from customers and stakeholders, and analyzing the collective

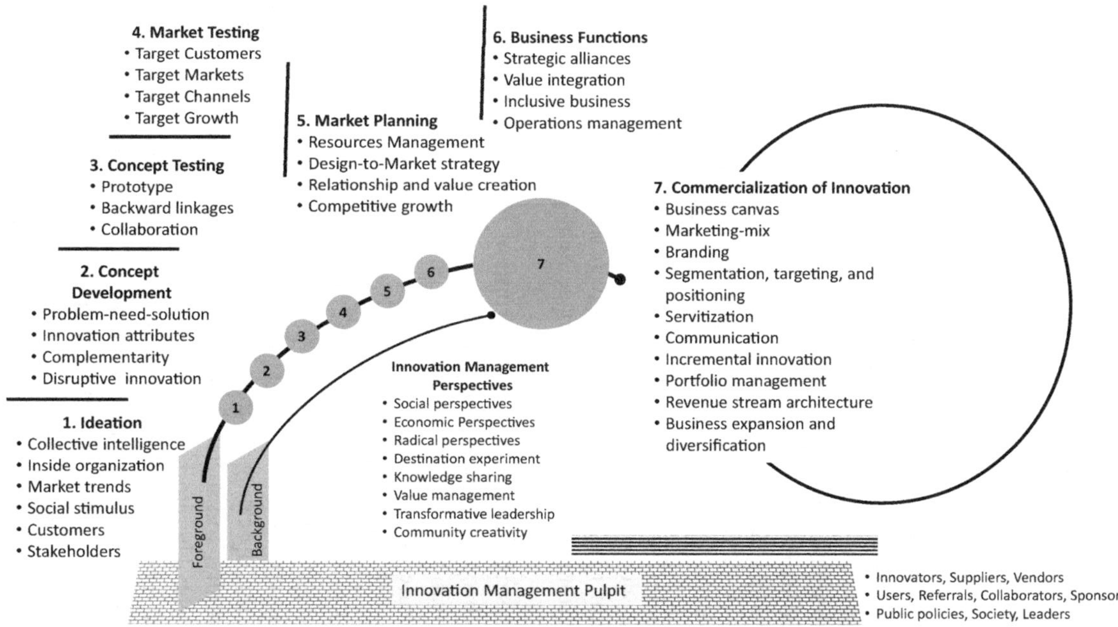

Fig. 5.2 Innovation management blueprint (*Source* Author)

intelligence inputs. Appropriate innovative ideas lead to concept development based on the analysis of triadic factors consisting of consumer problems, derived needs, and anticipated solutions. At this stage, the major challenge to the enterprises is to develop innovative attributes to make the innovation effective to the end users. The secondary ideas on innovation also emerge by analyzing the ideas complementary to the existing products (complementarity) and overriding disruptive innovations of short lifecycles.

The effective concept development of new innovations leads to the creation of prototypes, map backward linkages, and explore innovation collaborations. These factors are contextual to the third stage as *concept testing*. Upon successful development of prototypes, backward linkages, and innovation collaborations, the new innovations face the challenge of market testing to explore target customer, target markets, target channels, and prediction of business growth. The market planning to diffuse innovations needs mapping of resource management, creating design-to-market strategy (including go-to-market strategy), and ensuring customer relationship to create value. These factors of market planning help enterprises in systematically planning the competitive growth. In addition, innovation management needs to be supported by various functions, principally strategic alliances, across manufacturing, product design, technology, distribution, and finance. The strategic alliances also help in coordinating operations and supply chain management. The inclusive business approach allows customers and stakeholders to contribute to various business decisions to improve the functionality and value integration process. An appropriate integration of the above six stages of innovation management helps enterprises in increasing competitiveness and creating value-based advantages against disruptive innovations (Miles et al., 2018).

As the increasing inflow of radical innovations engulf the contemporary markets, it is challenging to micro- and small enterprises to commercialize their innovation and appropriately channelize thru the end user. Figure 5.2 highlights the commercialization of innovation needs to be blended within localized business canvas model (key partners, key activities, key resources, value propositions, customer relationships, channels, customer segments, cost structure, and revenue streams). Branding of local innovations is important to outreach the consumer segments and position the innovation as a commodity. In addition, successful innovations embed servitization benefits to manage the innovation portfolios successfully. The marketing mix for innovative products should be designed comprehensively with 11Ps comprising (Rajagopal, 2019):

- Product (attributes, perceived use value, product lifecycle)
- Price (value-based pricing)
- Place (multi-channel marketing)
- Promotion (need-based promotion)
- Packaging (sustainability)
- Pace (first-mover advantage)
- People (referrals, gatekeepers, customer relationship)
- Performance (product portfolio and product line performance)
- Psychodynamics (Interactive marketing, social media, and community networking)
- Posture (unique entrepreneurial identity), and
- Proliferation (disruption, diversification, digitalization).

Besides the above factors in managing innovations, the social and economic factors affect the localization of innovations. The radical perspectives in commercializing innovations often serve as competitive drivers to market innovations beyond niche. Most innovations are carried out by the micro and small enterprises as the destination experiments and face a major challenge in knowledge sharing and value management due to limitations in resources and leadership drive.

The growing trend of market innovation motivates micro and small enterprises to blend technology and marketing strategies to create unique contributions of innovations embedding desired customer values. It is essential for innovations to grow effective and stronger to resist the market competition and avoid the cannibalization by competing innovations. It has been observed that product innovations have a positive impact within the short and long term, which inculcates the customer value, posture of enterprise, revenues, and gross earnings. However, some reverse innovations initially generated by micro and small enterprises and commercialized by large enterprises generate high returns and low risk due to effective brand propagation (Pauwels et al., 2004; Sorescu & Spanjol, 2008). In addition, market-based innovations have positive effects on enterprises and product performance, while technology-based innovations have stronger effects on value creation and adaptability.

Collective Intelligence and Market Competitiveness

Crowd-based businesses evolve on collective intelligence in developing innovative products with utilitarian perspectives at a low cost to enable consumers to inculcate high perceived value. The enterprises engaged in open innovation attract crowd-based ideas and implement design thinking process in developing prototypes and their commercialization embedding consumer touchpoints including product attractiveness, price, affordable technology, and use value. The collective intelligence in business action helps entrepreneurial leaders and managers to systematically implement crowd ideation and features of product uniqueness to gain market competitiveness. The crowd involvement in designing innovative products in local enterprises has been boosted up through advancements in information technology and interactive marketing approaches using social media platforms effectively. The web-enabled collective intelligence has been the prime source of knowledge diffusion, adaptation, and practice since the inception of the twenty-first century. The diffusion of collective intelligence has helped micro and small enterprises to grow manifold with 3-dimensional management approach comprising advancements in frugal innovation (Y-axis: length), social needs emerged out of common community problems (X-axis: breadth), commercialization of innovation in the context of competitive pricing, utilitarian approach, and perceived use value (Z-axis: depth). Consequently, the growth of micro and small enterprises based on collective intelligence has emerged as a set of building blocks with various managerial permutations and combinations to gain competitive advantage and expand beyond the niche.

The active participation in social media channels have encouraged the micro and small enterprises not only to outsource the business activities but also to explore new business opportunities. These firms tend to develop crowd-based business models to gain competitive advantage through working with collective intelligence-based innovative ideas, prototypes, and business processes to capture customer value and gain market share. The involvement of the crowd in developing business models needs effective integration of contributors outside the enterprise and alignment with the entrepreneurial goals to streamline the innovation and business processes. The collective intelligence functions effectively on peer-to-peer platforms, where the contributors' values can be effectively integrated and transformed into key activities of business canvas (Kohler,

2015). The use of collective intelligence in micro and small enterprises tends to cocreate the innovation design and value with crowds by emphasizing the competitive market propositions. Commonly, the crowd-based ideations advocate low-cost, low-quality alternatives against the existing commercial brands with relatively higher quality and price. However, the low-cost and low-quality perceptions are altered by the users over time by sharing their experiences on social media channels. Consequently, the collective intelligence helps in building an effective innovation and business management system by mobilizing ideation and skills to enrich the innovation and business processes. Standardization of collective intelligence concepts poses a major challenge to many nascent enterprises, which requires a thorough review and checks of redundancy in ideas, duplication in business processes, cost overlaps, refining the use of technology, mass production, and commercialization of innovative products. Therefore, collective intelligence has both easy to acquire and hard to use perspectives in transforming ideas related to innovation and business processes. New ventures in emerging markets could capitalize on the crowd contributors to create and deliver value-based innovative products. However, such products succumb to a short life cycle and fail to resist the thrust of market competition. In an advanced contribution, the collective intelligence serves as a skill-sharing platform, which connects to local technocrats, leaders, and business managers who are proactive to develop and implement crowd-based business models (Kietzmann, 2017).

The collective intelligence-based companies largely derive business ideas either from face-to-face interactions within the community or through digital platforms. These firms exhibit the characteristics after reaching out innovative ideas beyond traditional boundaries and exploiting technologies through digital platforms. These attributes contribute to value creation and mapping the crowd semantics to opt for the most competitive solutions in conducting business. Firms based on collective intelligence tend to use shared resources and process collaborations in managing micro and macro tasks engaging stakeholders and customers. Therefore, the crowd-based business modeling encourages firms toward collective production and business operations against working with the conventional family-based entrepreneurial models (Kietzmann et al., 2011). Enterprises intending to cocreate values involving crowd culture are able to inculcate higher value propositions than conventional firms as crowd-based contents are often rich, diverse, and experience-based, which strengthens the enterprises to stand against competitors. In many developing countries like India and China, the micro and small enterprises are supported by systematically documented ideation- and business-process compendium, which is generated through collective intelligence. Such documents are provided by the governmental and non-governmental organizations to facilitate these enterprises and develop further connectivity with the community and crowd. Collective intelligence provides the real time distributed knowledge and enhances the skills among entrepreneurs to adapt to dynamic demand and trends of the market.

Skill sharing blended with technology and business management strategies have become a distinctive part of collective intelligence, which helps entrepreneurial learners understand the variety and relevance at the competitive marketplace. It is important for the enterprises to critically examine the collective information in the context of embedded crowd value to the firm and vice versa. In addition, firms also need to explore the tactics to meet specific challenges in the market such as disruption, shifts in consumer behavior, and hidden value advantages. Strategies responding to these challenging situations should be periodically assessed and refined to grow firms competitive and leverage their potential. The collective intelligence needs to be measured in the context of congruence of entrepreneurial objectives with crowd strategies, investment in collective intelligence, recurring cost of information acquisition, creation of crowd points, value propositions among contributors, risks associated with collective intelligence, and direct and indirect network effects. A systematic analysis of these parameters will ensure relationship between the firm, its size, and the universe of the crowd. The information acquired by refining crowd platforms is considered as crowd capital, which serves as an organizational resource in the development of business models, implementation, monitoring, and evaluation (Prpic et al., 2015).

The volume of information, attributes of information, and thematic specialization depend on the size of the crowd and its characteristics. The characteristics of the crowd reflect in the ideation and strategy effects. It's observed that a strong positive crowd network contributes to effective strategies than short-term tactics. Enterprises using collective intelligence need to invest in the crowd by segmenting them to selective platforms and analyzing the contents of collective intelligence. Therefore, enterprises need to invest in creating their own platforms, information research needs, and managing crowd activities (human capital). In addition, the recurring cost of information acquisition, storage, and digital infrastructure also needs to be planned by the enterprises intending to use collective intelligence. The unfiltered crowd information is often chaotic. Therefore, specialized parameters need to be developed for information acquisitions in both text and visual modes. The cost of information stored in data and image formats tends to increase periodically. The relationship between time and quality of information also needs to be filtered in temporal intervals and information should be arrayed using various parameters like theme, contents, period (temporal), destinations (spatial), technology, and effective public policies. Appropriate use of collective information helps companies in trendy branding, the managing scale of economies, establishing a bridge between conventional word-of-mouth, and digital dispersion of information. The creation of crowd points and sharing of value propositions among contributors is an essential organizational process to ensure the quality of information, reduce associated risks, and negative effects of indirect networks (Franzoni & Sauermann, 2014). The attributes of collective intelligence and market competitiveness in a cloud environment are illustrated in Fig. 5.3.

The cloud environment has supported effective functionality of collective intelligence on various social media channels, which enables crowd participation to explore open innovation within society and in engagement with customer-centric and business-to-business companies. Figure 5.3 illustrates that the crowd participation on any open innovation concept based on social needs often turns chaotic unless the crowd segmentation is done by social institutions or companies to explore collective intelligence. The segmented crowd participation tends to focus on predefined perspectives on ideation, innovation, and marketing approaches. The focused participation of the crowd also helps in managing crowd-based business and social enterprise projects through developing collective ideation and process mapping for effective implementation and collective audit. To involve crowd participation on social needs, it is necessary for social institutions identify clear problems.

Well-established needs of the society help in generating collective intelligence and community consciousness. Diffusion of collective intelligence on social need-based solutions drives social consumption behavior over time. The crowd participation and community support in managing social needs and providing effective solutions to social problems encourage co-creation, direct communications, and inclusivity (involvement of people). Cocreation and development of inclusive entrepreneurial model helps

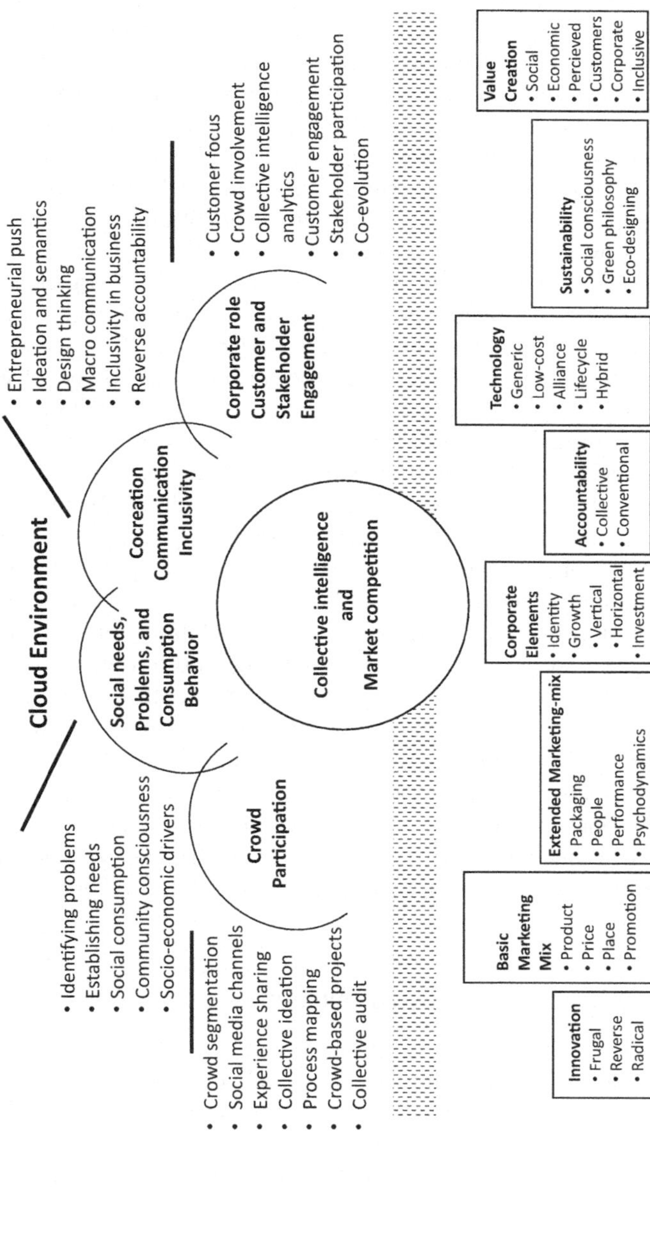

Fig. 5.3 Collective intelligence and market competition (*Source* Author)

micro and small enterprises to develop a unique corporate identity to gain market competitiveness. The mapping of ideation and semantics emerging out of crowd participation helps in design thinking. Collective intelligence can be considered as a macro communication platform, which blends business ideas, strategies, and competitive interventions to drive enterprises beyond niche markets. The inclusivity in business significantly encourages people's audit in enterprises as reverse accountability. Inclusive business and crowd participation are contextual in enhancing entrepreneurial capability which drives the expansion of entrepreneurial activities and improves their quality of life. Collective intelligence platforms are supported by social institutions, non-governmental organizations, and stakeholders to encourage small scale sectors in developing business value chains (Chamberlain & Anseeuw, 2019). Therefore, crowd involvement with customer and stakeholder focus is essential to coevolve enterprises. Companies play a significant role in collective intelligence analytics and managing systematic engagement of customers to gain market competitiveness. Collective intelligence affects the market competition in the context of innovations (frugal, reverse, radical) promoted through basic marketing mix of 4Ps comprising product, price, place, and promotion. In addition, the collective intelligence also helps in developing new packaging ideas, public inputs for vertical and horizontal growth of the enterprise, and exploring the possibilities of crowdfunding. Enterprises supported by crowdsourcing and crowdfunding lean toward collective accountability against the conventional control mechanism. The crowd participation also helps enterprises in identifying low-cost technology and improving the generic technologies for augmenting performance of products and services and critically examining the conventional life cycles. Crowd-based enterprises also manage the entrepreneurial sustainability perspectives successfully, like cocreating the green philosophy and engaging people in eco-designing of products and services.

Challenges and Prospects

Amidst the chaos of entrepreneurial performance in micro and small enterprises across developing economies, many challenges emerge toward establishing new ventures, streamlining the operations of existing ventures, and creating sustainable value chains. Many enterprises have experimented with a new route to success by acquiring small businesses as an *acquisition entrepreneurship* strategy. This strategy involves buying an existing enterprise and continuing its operations until the new plans are established to gain a competitive advantage. In buying and running existing enterprises, it's important to thoroughly examine the assets, liabilities, and business prospects associated with the enterprise. These factors need to be refined through critical thinking, expert opinions, and simulated models to determine the managerial skills, customer confidence, the persuasiveness of enterprise, continuous learning, projected performance, and tolerance for stress and risk associated in carrying out entrepreneurial operations. In addition, the complementarity of entrepreneurial activities of the acquired portfolios needs to be simulated to project entrepreneurial performance on the basis of a rolling plan designed with periodicity (quarterly, half-yearly, yearly). The acquired enterprises need to be streamlined in reference to anticipated production and business operations and expected profit. During this phase, entrepreneurs need to ensure the flow of working capital, supplementary finance, and search for potential investors. Passing this stage, entrepreneurs may prepare to strike a deal in buying the existing enterprise and completing the legal formalities. Upon owning a functional enterprise, it is necessary to work on smooth transition in leadership. Accordingly, the organizational design and priorities need to be established to restructure relationships with employees, stakeholders, and market players (contract manufacturers, suppliers, promotors, and customer service providers). This is a critical stage as enterprises often spend imprudently on the acquired enterprises and develop cash flow crunch without ensuring the sources of funds (Ruback & Yudkoff, 2017).

One of the basic challenges in managing the acquired enterprises is to provide appropriate leadership and employee relationship. The centralized leadership, which is very common in micro and small enterprises, might not prove to be a good strategy to manage the acquired enterprises. Contrary to this, team strategy in managing the acquired enterprises appears to be a good option as pooled talents help in organization redesigning and establishing collective workstations with volunteered accountability and autonomous approach to achieve the established goals (Reich, 1987). In managing the existing enterprises or new ventures, it is necessary for entrepreneurs to be visionary, predicting the prospects of the enterprise, potential threats from new entrants, substitution effects, and bargaining power of suppliers and customers toward the existing product portfolios and services. Accordingly, the entrepreneurial leaders can develop defensive strategies, to reduce the impact from such operational disruptions. At the same time, an aggressive strategy to lead in a competitive marketplace would be helpful for micro and small enterprises. This strategy requires a creative push in production, marketing, and services by thrusting frugal innovative products, exploring low-end markets, price promotions, collaborative distribution, and generating effective psychodynamics through social media channels and customer advocacy. The creative enterprise's encourage crowd ideation, consortium production, and team marketing strategies to reap quick business results. The thorough face lifting of entrepreneurial strategies requires agile personality traits, which enable them to develop suitable alliances to work in varied business situations. The agility in personality traits can be managed by delegating the organizational and operations control to teams and creating a sense of trust and encourage collective applause for integrated efforts in holistic change management in enterprises to gain competitive leverage.

Despite the attributes of aggressive and defensive entrepreneurship, most entrepreneurs, especially women at the bottom-of-the-pyramid segment, suffer from social anxiety and economic deprivation in managing head-on challenges. Consequently, the lifecycle of micro and small enterprises is jeopardized and tends to succumb to social and business challenges. Entrepreneurs are required to remove structural barriers and reduce the objective risk of failure in enterprises. Most enterprises face failures because of conventional wisdom, and business ideas founded on short-sighted goals. Commonly, failures occur because of non-coordination between employees, strategic partners, and investors. In addition, ignoring feedbacks from potential customers and validating concepts with real customers on conventional settings disrupts the entrepreneurial growth and narrows down the profitability and upward mobility of products and services. Enterprises often suffer from fundamental attribution error by inappropriately emphasizing the relationship between leader, employees, and stakeholders, which causes disruption in decisions. Micro and small enterprises should adapt to lean enterprise culture by promoting flexible leadership, team and technical agility, developing innovative products, and creating demand in the market to deliver them to potential customers. This strategy helps in maintaining a zero inventory base by reducing the transaction cost. The competency of lean entrepreneurial design benefits the organization with emotional intelligence, communication skills, team efforts, and decentralization of decisions for attending to the market needs and generating quick responses. However, these enterprises need to protect themselves from falling into the velocity traps while approaching to meet attractive business opportunities. Such situations stimulate the entrepreneurs to adapt to myopic strategies by increasing prices, or compromising with the quality to sell at relatively lower prices than competitors to gain quick revenues. Such velocity traps in business often have kick-back effects as customer defection and diminishing brand value, which affects in customer acquisitions and forward collaborations with potential companies to drive business in the *big middle* segment.

Besides challenges, the new prospects of enterprises in developing economies include disruptive innovations and customer-centric, price-sensitive products. Investing in such innovations has emerged as a principal driver to create entrepreneurial wealth and foster inclusive and sustainable enterprises. These entrepreneurs tend to develop customer-centric businesses blending conventional wisdom with contemporary needs. Such blended products succeed in markets as ethnic products with technological backup. These products are identified as creative innovations with market focus and they attract the unmet local needs. Most fashion products and trendy home-furnishing products fall in this category, which has an ethnic touch and is based on the design supported by technological platforms. These products have a high price regime and have the potential to be positioned in the premium niche. In developing countries, trendy enterprises follow consortium production to set their businesses in the premium segment. These enterprises also enjoy social gains as they employ local artisans to manufacture products with contemporary designs using computer-aided designing technology (CAD). The market-based innovations provide a strong economic foundation, which not only creates consistent value chains, but also ensures profitability before growth. Consequently, the market-based innovations are commercialized with low capital investment in local markets, which exhibit the potential socioeconomic gains in terms of profit, employment, and boost in the local economy. Such innovations include contemporary designs, ethnic advertisement, low-end market promotions, restricted sales, and local distribution (Christensen et al., 2019). To attract angel investors on market-based entrepreneurial innovation projects, a clear project charter with summarized milestones should be developed in the context of real-time needs and market trends. Consequently, entrepreneurs should develop innovations for the shared value by meeting society's needs with an objective to build a profitable enterprise. Embedding social purpose in innovation needs a clear map of social problems, needs, and market trends. This determines a comprehensive view of social problems to identify appropriate customer targets. Most ethnic products, which belong to trendy fashion array, have the potential to be positioned in the premium segment by developing an attractive brand and associating it with celebrity endorsements like Shyam Ahuja Silks—an ethnic fashion company of India, which exports silk apparels under celebrity fashion banners. Moving to open markets with ethnic innovation leads to shared value, which helps in achieving business and social goals.

References

Asian Development Bank. (2016). *How inclusive is inclusive business for Women: Examples from Asia and Latin America*. Asian Development Bank.

Boland, R. J., Jr., & Tenkasi, R. (1995). Perspective making and perspective taking in communities of knowing. *Organization Science, 6*(4), 350–372.

Chamberlain, W., & Anseeuw, W. (2019). Inclusiveness revisited: Assessing inclusive businesses in South African agriculture. *Development Southern Africa, 36*(5), 600–615.

Christensen, C. M., Ojomo, E., & Dillon, K. (2019). *Cracking frontier markets*. Harvard Business Review Digital Article. Harvard Business School Press.

Edelman, D. C., & Singer, M. (2015, August). Competing on customer journeys. *Harvard Business Review*, 1–11.

England, D., Descartes, L., & Collier-Meek, M. (2011). Gender role portrayal and the Disney princesses. *Sex Roles, 64*(7/8), 555–567.

Florida, R., Cushing, R., & Gates, G. (2002). When social capital stifles innovation. *Harvard Business Review, 80*(8), 1–20.

Florida, R., & Goodnight, J. (2005). Managing for creativity. *Harvard Business Review, 83*(7), 124–131.

Franzoni, C., & Sauermann, H. (2014). Crowd science: The organization of scientific research in open collaborative projects. *Research Policy, 43*(1), 1–20.

Hearn, J., & Hein, W. (2015). Reframing gender and feminist knowledge construction in marketing and consumer research: Missing feminisms and the case of men and masculinities. *Journal of Marketing Management, 31*(15/16), 1626–1651.

Jarvenpaa, S. L., & Välikangas, L. (2014). Opportunity creation in innovation networks: Interactive revealing practices. *California Management Review, 57*(1), 67–87.

Kohler, T. (2015). Crowdsourcing-based business models: How to create and capture value. *California Management Review, 57*(4), 63–84.

Kietzmann, J. H. (2017). Crowdsourcing: A revised definition and an introduction to new research. *Business Horizons, 60*(2), 151–153.

Kietzmann, J. H., Hermkens, K., McCarthy, I. P., & Silvestre, B. S. (2011). Social media? Get serious! Understanding the functional building blocks of social media. *Business Horizons, 54*(3), 241–251.

Ladge, J., Eddleston, K. A., & Sugiyama, K. (2019). Am I an entrepreneur? How imposter fears hinder women entrepreneurs' business growth. *Business Horizons, 62*(5), 615–624.

Langer, E., & Beard, A. (2014). Mindfulness in the age of complexity. *Harvard Business Review, 92*(3), 68–73.

Liedtka, J. M. (2018). *Why design thinking works*. Harvard Business Review Digital Article. Harvard Business School Press.

Luqman, A., Talwar, S., Masood, A., & Dhir, A. (2021). Does enterprise social media use promote employee creativity and well-being? *Journal of Business Research, 131*, 40–54.

Miles, I., Belousova, V., & Chichkanov, N. (2018). Knowledge intensive business services: Ambiguities and continuities. *Foresight, 20*(1), 1–26.

Montgomery, C. A. (2008). Putting leadership back into strategy. *Harvard Business Review, 86*(1), 54–60.

Murray, J. B., Brokalaki, Z., Bhogal-Nair, A., Cermin, A., Chelekis, J., & Cocker, H. (2019). Toward a processual theory of transformation. *Journal of Business Research, 100*(7), 319–326.

Pauwels, K., Silva-Risso, J., Srinivasan, S., & Hanssens, D. M. (2004). New products, sales promotions, and firm value: The case of the automobile industry. *Journal of Marketing, 68*(4), 142–156.

Prpić, J., Shukla, P. P., Kietzmann, J. H., & McCarthy, I. P. (2015). How to work a crowd: Developing crowd capital through crowdsourcing. *Business Horizons, 58*(1), 77–85.

Rajagopal, A. (2019). *Contemporary marketing strategy: Analyzing consumer behavior to drive managerial decision making*. Palgrave Macmillan.

Rajagopal, A. (2021a). *The business design cube: Converging markets, society, and customer values to grow competitive in business*. Business Expert Press.

Rajagopal, A. (2021b). *Crowd-based business models—Using collective intelligence for market competitiveness*. Palgrave Macmillan.

Reich, R. B. (1987). Entrepreneurship reconsidered: The team as hero. *Harvard Business Review*, 1–20.

Ruback, R. S., & Yudkoff, R. (2017, January–February). Buying your way into entrepreneurship. *Harvard Business Review*, 149–153.

Saebi, T., Foss, N. J., & Linder, S. (2019). Social entrepreneurship research: Past achievements and future promises. *Journal of Management, 45*(1), 70–95.

Schiele, K., Louie, L., & Chen, S. (2020). Marketing feminism in youth media: A study of Disney and Pixar animation. *Business Horizons, 63*(5), 659–669.

Sorescu, A. B., & Spanjol, J. (2008). Innovation's effect on firm value and risk: Insights from consumer-packaged goods. *Journal of Marketing, 72*(2), 114–132.

Valcárcel, A. (2002). *The collective memory and challenges of feminism*. Women and Child Development Unit. Economic Commission for Latin America and Caribbean, United Nations, Santiago, Chile.

Wilson, K., & Doz, Y. L. (2012). 10 Rules for managing global innovation. *Harvard Business Review, 90*(10), 84–90.

CHAPTER 6

Learning from Experience

Abstract This chapter presents an appraisal of entrepreneurial practices followed by women entrepreneurs across developing countries. The chapter includes contemporary entrepreneurial practices of five major developing economies (Mexico, Brazil, India, Africa, and China) emphasizing the attributes of women leadership, business capabilities, technological competencies, and managing collective intelligence. General discussions on comparison of attributes and entrepreneurial practices across different destinations have been covered in this chapter.

Keyword Global perspectives · Women entrepreneurs · India · Mexico · Africa · Brazil · China

Developing economies have been engaged in social and economic transformation since long. However, the pace of economic transition is slow due to the limitations of infrastructure, financial resources, and innovation motivations in developing countries. Women entrepreneurs in Asia broadly comprising of China and India have shown significant growth in micro and small enterprises within manufacturing and services sectors. Women entrepreneurs in India make significant contributions through micro, small, and medium enterprises which have improved the regional

A. Rajagopal, *Women Entrepreneurs in Emerging Markets*, International Marketing and Management Research,
https://doi.org/10.1007/978-3-030-89770-3_6

and national entrepreneurial earning over the years. Collectively, women-owned enterprises play a crucial role in alleviating poverty by generating regular household income, which significantly affects the social values and quality of life. Women entrepreneurs in India are recognized as consortium workers to implement public policies and as a client group for establishing forward linkages such as supply chain, marketing, and international commerce. Most women enterprises in India are engaged in services, while a small segment is working with the manufacturing of food products, textile, local cosmetics, and fashion accessories like leather products. Despite various economic programs supported by the public policies in developing countries, the per capita income has not grown to a desired level and most micro and small enterprises face shortage of working capital as compared to the mainstream manufacturing and service enterprises (Premchender, 2003). This chapter illustrates public policies and the state of art of micro and small women enterprises in India, Mexico, China, Africa, and Brazil.

Women Enterprises in India

Indian rural economy is transforming continuously by upgrading the infrastructure, resources, technology, and management skills in micro and small enterprises led by women. However, the macroeconomic policies concerning structural reforms have yet to penetrate the rural economy and provide a conducive environment for women-led micro and small enterprises. Resource availability through public programs in India requires state contributions also, which vary according to the financial status of respective states. The public policies have significantly stimulated the public and private sector financial institutions to provide necessary resources for the entrepreneurs at the grassroots to establish new ventures and improve the operational capacity of the existing entrepreneurial firms. The capital subsidy under entrepreneurial development programs and flexibility in payback period has encouraged investment and productivity gains in the rural farm and non-farm sectors. In addition, the Fintec companies evaluate the entrepreneurial projects and provide financial resources and technical guidance based on the proposed innovation and use of technology.

The encouragement of women entrepreneurship in India has achieved a significant lead in assuring gender equality by reducing the social discrimination against women and empowering them to gain economic liberty. The role of self-help groups and regional non-governmental organizations is also proactive in developing women entrepreneurship by providing technical and managerial skills in addition to the collective finance schemes. The government-led prioritization of women entrepreneurship has benefitted the economic grassroots movement of self-help groups and civil society organizations to provide financial linkages, marketing linkages, and awareness initiatives around public policies and government schemes, which have enabled capacity building, manufacturing design training, and soft skills in managing enterprises independently by women (Patnaik, 2021).

Women enterprises at the bottom of the pyramid have been guided by the social institutions including self-help groups to use social media extensively and seek leverage of crowd ideation and crowdfunding to manage entrepreneurial resources. Besides the crowd-based support and collective intelligence, the government-supported social institutions like Council for Advancement of Peoples Action and Rural Technology help women entrepreneurs to develop generic technologies and access the low-cost technologies to improve the performance of their enterprises. Some public sector organizations in farm and non-farm sectors such as Regional Handloom Cooperative Societies and Coir Board have developed generic technologies for manufacturing and designing products. State-sponsored handloom societies have improved the production infrastructure of weavers dominated by female workers by transforming pit-looms to power looms. Similarly, the Coir Board is engaged in encouraging women entrepreneurs to manufacture various utilitarian products using coconut fiber. The Coir Board has designed generic automatic power loom to make the production and maintenance easy and low cost. In addition, the sectoral institutions, public and private financial institutions, and self-help groups are committed to providing microloans to finance the business needs of women entrepreneurs irrespective of the size and volume of production. Most women enterprises in India are located in the non-farm sector with concentration on services, as manufacturing activity is too complex to be managed by women entrepreneurs.

In addition to for-profit women enterprises, women are also engaged in social enterprises, in health and education sector with an objective to improve quality of life, generate contemporary values, and uplift socioeconomic status of the target segment. One of such social enterprise has been founded in 1994 as Udayan Care, which is committed to raising orphans in a family environment and reintegrate them into the social environment by providing a conducive home environment under *Udayan Ghar* program. This enterprise has evolved around National Capital Region and spread over 10 cities since 2015. This social enterprise serves as not-for-profit entity with social objectives of nurturing and educating socioeconomically deprived children and youth in India, and offers employment to several women and inculcates entrepreneurial skills in them. In manufacturing enterprises, an innovative cooler evolved from its generic design of double-walled clay pot with water-lining in between the walls, which serves as a conventional cooler for low-income families. This conventional cooler serves as a sustainable refrigerator with the capacity to retain the food fresh for 72 h. On the premise of this design, the Godrej & Boyce manufacturing company developed a portable non-compressor cooler, which is suitable for cooling beverage cans. This is a hybrid innovation co-created on the local entrepreneurial design and commercialized as a reverse innovation. There are many locally organized women-led microfinance enterprises that encourage women to save money out of their disposable income. These microfinance institutions locally known as Chit Funds are operated within the agglomeration of households, and all operations are controlled by women ensuring the availability of funds to the members in need. A large women-led organization known as Self-Employed Women's Association (SEWA) works to improve the quality of life of poor rural and urban women in India by engaging them in various creative manufacturing and commercial activities such as ethnic jewelry, ethnic products out of inorganic waste materials, and rag-pickers artifacts. This social enterprise has expanded over the years and established a trade facilitation center, which provides training to women entrepreneurs on soft skills, ethnic designs, ethnic fashion, and home furnishings. This center provides convergence of traditional embroidery skills with contemporary apparel and home furnishings and markets these products through agents in different parts of the world specifically in Europe. This center is organized as women entrepreneur's cooperative, which is owned by the artisan members. This center has transformed into a for-profit enterprise to reinvest its profits in sustainable growth and access external resources (capital and technology), which allows the center to provide higher dividends to the artisan members. The supply chain to support the manufacturing process is based on a consortium model, which demonstrates production across village workers and the centralized facility to design new products and various steps involved in cutting, stitching, and embroidery. The member artisans are guided about finishing the products, and the center provides assembled kits containing raw material and production tools with deadlines to complete the task. The products are collected and pre-scheduled transports are arranged. However, the trade facilitating center has undergone several competitive pressures from the business organizations engaged in the marketing of ethnic and artisanal products within the Indian market. The brand name of the ethnic product was determined as Hansiba, which was extended to Western and fusion-style clothing. These products are largely distributed through large retail chain stores such as Fab India and smaller stores serving the big middle class. These products are sold at par with contemporary fashion products at relatively higher prices in the above chain stores (Khaire & McGinn, 2010).

Creative Community in Mexico

The situation of entrepreneurs in Mexico is not very different from the Indian scenario as far as the individual entrepreneurs are concerned. There are many artisanal communities across states in Mexico, which are engaged in developing ethnic products and promoting them within the niche market. These entrepreneurs exhibit an economic orientation toward marketing ethnic products for generating income to support livelihood. Most entrepreneurs have learned skills as family business. Entrepreneurs in Mexico largely face financial resource crunch, which affects their entrepreneurial growth, as there is no vertical growth for entrepreneurial products in niche and urban markets. The microfinance institutions tend to support local artisans with limited financial resources to carry out their production operations. However, most entrepreneurs are deprived of private market finance due to the lack of collateral assets. A few entrepreneurs could develop entrepreneurial firms with collaboration of export agents who provided low-cost technology, financial resources, and minimum infrastructures to manufacture products. With the above facilities, the women entrepreneurs are engaged in non-farm entrepreneurial activities including ethnic textile and apparel, pottery, wooden toys, and souvenirs. Mexico is largely dominated by tourism-based entrepreneurship, which has a potential market for ethnic products and souvenirs.

Jugaré, an innovative educational toy enterprise in Mexico, is committed to children's development through a creative place with focus on establishing convergence between parents and children. This enterprise started with a small capital outlay and manufacturing agenda to provide educational toys for children at affordable prices through local retail channels. However, this enterprise has faced strong competition from international manufacturers such as LEGO, which has diminished the value of its toys despite embedded creativity. Apart from international brands, the other educational toy firms include Alex Toys, Juguetes Nip, and Imaginarium. Imaginarium has its own chain stores at large shopping malls in various cities in Mexico. This company also distributes supplementary material such as children's furniture for playing toys. The price of Imginarium brand products are relatively higher than Jugaré's, as consumers prefer complementary products and gaming infrastructure to provide a complete set for their children. Due to limitations of finance and production infrastructure, it was hard for Jugaré enterprise to reach the breakeven point. However, after marginal success in the early days, the enterprise has decided to appoint franchisees for fast expansion and marketing within the country. This brief case study of Jugaré's emphasizes on limitations of resources faced by creative enterprises, which further moves to the competition grid of local and international brands affecting the brand equity and brand performance (Brambila et al., 2013).

Women entrepreneurs in Mexico grow out of the family business. While struggling for independent leadership, women in Mexico face major challenges to overcome social stigma and the masculinity effect. However, their husbands or boyfriends constitute significant support for women entrepreneurs followed by parents and other family members. Most women entrepreneurs in Mexico begin their entrepreneurial activity as a start-up enterprise with an innate focus of owning a business, improving lifestyle, and establishing independence as principal drivers. Besides social and personality factors, women entrepreneurs in Mexico are deeply concerned about achieving economic empowerment despite family and social problems. Talavera de la Reyna is an enterprise of a women entrepreneur in Puebla, Mexico, which combines the traditional pottery with Spanish pottery designs. This blend of pottery has an aesthetic value in Mexico and it is a tourist attraction. This enterprise manufactures pottery using an organic and sustainable manufacturing process. The ceramic designs of this pottery are tin glassed, which incorporates the elements of porcelain. Talavera de la Reyna has adapted the way of blending business art and sustainable activities. Over time, this enterprise has owned a Talavera showroom called ALARCA to reinforce the social values among millennials and attract tourism. This is one-of-a-kind showroom in Latin America. Though this enterprise has experienced several years of success, the lead women entrepreneur of this company had undergone several social and family-based complexities, which has affected the work-life balance during the early days of entrepreneurship. Women entrepreneurs require persistence, awareness of growth perspectives, and competence to manage personal and entrepreneurial obstacles. Over time, Talavera de la Reyna received government recognition and certification for the Talavera craft, which established that this pottery is unique and ecologically sustainable (Rajagopal et al., 2013).

Lindahermosa is a fashion brand from Yucatán, Mexico that offers accessories handmade by local artisan women to promote their talent and benefit their homes and communities. This women-led enterprise is organized on the principles of consortium production, which emphasizes collective manufacturing but centralized branding and marketing activity. The entrepreneurs use ethnic material to develop fashion accessories, which are centrally designed by the lead entrepreneur of Lindahermosa. The lead entrepreneur distributes design and raw materials to the local entrepreneurs who return the finished products as per schedule for internal processing in terms of pricing, promotion, packaging, and delivery. The products of Lindahermosa constitute weaving, embroidery, and cross-stitch among others, which are based on creative designs. The major markets for these products are the tourism centers in Yucatan state and Cancun city. Handmade cross-stitch clothes have become a very popular trend, due to which, local retail outlets have promoted these products. These products are locally classified as sustainable and slow-fashion products. Besides destination retailing, this enterprise has also expanded to delivering ethnic fashion products through mail order and online transactions. Since this enterprise is located in a tourism hub, it has experienced long lean seasons and short peak seasons. In general, ethnic enterprises in Mexico and Latin America are strongly related to tourism potential. Ethnic products do not have a strong domestic market but export agents in Mexico have promoted these products in Europe and the United States significantly (Lecuna et al., 2017).

Entrepreneurial Ventures in Africa

The entrepreneurship in South Africa is of a mixed portfolio comprising farm and non-farm enterprises organized in the forms of individual, collective, and alliance enterprises. Most women entrepreneurs are engaged in the services sector, while men dominate the production sector where women entrepreneurs also serve as associates in production and business operations. A large number of farm-based enterprises are engaged in on-form activities due to a large number of smallholdings. These enterprises contribute to improving the standard of living of rural poor who are dependent on smallholder agricultural sector in an irrigated farming segment. These farmer entrepreneurs are supported by public policies, which aims to integrate subsistence form income with commercial agricultural economy by exploring new entrepreneurial ventures. Therefore, developing rural entrepreneurship has become more of a natural choice than a public policy or commercial alliance to benefit the rural poor by improving the per capita income, quality of life, employment, and interface with the business environment. While driving small farm enterprises, the entrepreneurs encounter information gap and several risk-averse situations despite the spirit to meet hard challenges within society and economy. It has been observed in previous studies that the male entrepreneurs having marginal and small landholdings dominate the farm enterprises as compared to their female counterparts, which illustrates the gender bias in rural communities. However, the female farmer entrepreneurs are also engaged marginally in farm enterprises but they largely operate with lower aspirations (Wale et al., 2021).

Most farm enterprises in South Africa operate in collective action groups, which enables farmer entrepreneurs to earn higher income as compared to women entrepreneurs. However, these entrepreneurs face limitations in resources and infrastructure about farm irrigation and credit for agricultural inputs. Farm entrepreneurship in South Africa is largely based on demand-driven farming supported by extension services, market linkages, and access to finance which helps in improving the per capital household income of farmers. The informal microcredit infrastructure also supports the farmer entrepreneurs and contributes to improving agricultural production, marketing, and value chain in the entrepreneurial process. In farm enterprises, women farmers face challenges in acquiring agricultural information regarding inputs, prices, markets, and financial services. The microfinance services are largely community-oriented and operate on informal roles set within the member groups or community (Nagler & Naudé, 2017; Wale et al., 2021).

Female entrepreneurs in Africa have established a long tradition through ethnic products in the non-farm enterprise segment. These products have reached European and American markets beyond the confined niche. Some women entrepreneurs in Africa are phenomenal such as Maggy Lawson, locally known in Togo as Mama Benz, who has popularized entrepreneurship in the fashion apparel segment by selling the brightly printed cotton cloth throughout Western Africa (Dieterich et al., 2016). Similarly, many women entrepreneurs rose into prominence by sheer dint of their merit. Women entrepreneurs in Africa are synonymous with business as they contribute significantly to the regional economy and transformation of social values and lifestyle. Their contributions can be acknowledged in innovation, creating employment, poverty elimination, household financial upliftment, and social wealth creation. Many countries in Africa have experienced a systematic and gradual rise in female entrepreneurship over the twentieth century. Arguably, the contribution of women entrepreneurs in the African continent has been discussed in various research studies, which exhibit mixed results in entrepreneurial performance across the countries in Africa. Exploring profitable entrepreneurial opportunities is a consistent need largely influenced by political and social factors. At the microlevel, most entrepreneurs draw individual resources and explore the possibilities of external resources through public programs or private alliances (Ojong et al., 2021).

Women entrepreneurs in South Africa have various motivations to start an enterprise such as the family concerns, self-determination, economic empowerment, liberation from discrimination, career advancements, organizational dynamics, and entrepreneurial power. In addition, women entrepreneurs venture into economic activities to contribute to the household, personal, and social income to a large extent. These entrepreneurs face many sociocultural constraints, which lead them to distress and untoward experiences in operating enterprises. Such situations diminish the venture dynamics and socioeconomic value, which impedes women's accessibility to resources and strategic alliances. The effective networking and the support of local social institutions and international organizations have brought umbrella effect in women entrepreneurship by encouraging collective efforts in managing enterprises and seeking support on entrepreneurial resources within and outside the destination. However, women entrepreneurs in Africa need stronger emotional support to encourage them to manage multiple production and marketing tasks through multichannel networks. Despite government and non-governmental encouragement, a large segment of women tends to operate in microenterprises within niche. There is a need for encouragement for women entrepreneurs to adapt to consortium production and establish business alliances with large companies and retailers for the marketing of ethnic products. However, these entrepreneurs encounter technological, managerial, and marketing problems during the transition from conventional wisdom enterprise to contemporary, collective, or digital intelligence enterprise (Henry et al., 2016).

Most artisanal and small-scale enterprises in Sub-Saharan Africa are characterized by low technology and labor-intensive enterprises. Artisanal entrepreneurs largely operate in non-farm enterprises and significantly contribute to household income and employment. There are many pull and push factors that motivate artisanal entrepreneurs in the region. Accordingly, there is an inter-sectoral migration between farm and non-farm enterprises. Exploring income-generating opportunities during the lean season acts as a principal pull factor. Meeting the essential needs in low-income families and overcoming the negative socioeconomic shocks stimulate the artisans to push against the situation and drive entrepreneurship with business motivation. The lower credit markets often create compulsion among entrepreneurs to market their products at low prices despite high ethnic value to generate subsistence income and generate own capital for future investment in an enterprise. However, family firms, which invest their own capital, are susceptible to high-risk environment within the limited social security and neighborhood protection. Despite the low turnover in artisanal products within niche market, the household members are thrust to entrepreneurship. Consequently, families put pressure to manage both farm and non-farm entrepreneurial activities by administering their own finances to facilitate niche-based entrepreneurship (Ackah, 2013; Nagler & Naudé, 2017).

South Africa's constitutional and legislative framework has been very sensitive to women's empowerment and gender equality. The Broad Based Black Economic Empowerment Act promotes women entrepreneurs to manage new enterprises by increasing their access to new economic activities, community infrastructure, and skill development programs. The public policies in South Africa are committed to enhancing the financial literacy among women, their attitudes toward banking, awareness about development finance, and exploring opportunities for advanced entrepreneurship. Such policy and community push help women to move up the business ladder and explore new entrepreneurial opportunities in the services and manufacturing sector. Microfinance has been considered as an important source for women's economic empowerment, and two major microenterprise companies Marang Financial Services and Small Enterprise Foundation are engaged in exploring the underserviced areas to provide financial support to artisanal entrepreneurs. The impact of microfinance in Sub-Saharan Africa has significantly affected women's empowerment, housing, employment, and social cohesion despite the risks of refinance and payback (van Rooyen et al., 2012).

Entrepreneurship at Grassroots in Brazil

Unexceptionally, women entrepreneurs have contributed significantly to the economic growth and employment in Brazil like in other developing countries. Women entrepreneurs in Brazil are largely evolved from family businesses and family-related economic context, which have motivated them to adapt to business environment and strike a work-life balance. Brazilian women entrepreneurs manage their enterprises with 5 M concerns comprising marketing push, monetary gains, micromanagement, motherhood, and motivations derived from the community. Female entrepreneurs operate in different socioeconomic contexts across Brazil, which are largely affected by family, fraternity, and freedom in society. These factors determine the behavioral perspective of female entrepreneurs like in many integrated cultures. As observed in developing economies, family financial support is a strong, tangible, valuable, and indispensable factor to evolve business ventures in a competitive marketplace. Women in Brazil draw significant emotional support from the family in managing micro and small enterprises within niche markets and consider family as a social capital (Kaciak & Welsh, 2020). Most women entrepreneurs in Brazil are engaged in the services sector within the beauty and fashion segment. These entrepreneurs aspire to establish chain stores instead of focusing on micro-outlets of services. The beauty segment includes a chain of hairdressing and beauty saloons with afro hair design. The women entrepreneurs in Brazil have a market-oriented mindset, and they experiment competitive strategies through interpersonal communications and media campaigns, pushing business through promotional strategies, and broadening the services offerings. These entrepreneurs accept challenges and orient their entrepreneurial growth with for-profit and value propositions. Similarly, Beleza Natural, a Brazilian chain of beauty institutes, operates in international destinations in Latin America with both men and women in the workforce. This enterprise focuses on giving women facelift with curly and wavy hair designs through a franchise business model by engaging local workforces in various destinations (Besbes et al., 2012).

Social relationships among women entrepreneurs in Brazil influence entrepreneurial operations both internally and externally. They also face role conflicts as an entrepreneur and a family manager. The business–family interface significantly affects the entrepreneurial operations and the gender role perspective, as both are intertwined and affect the work-life balance among women entrepreneurs. Commonly, the gender roles within the traditional household lead to internal conflict and stress over the entrepreneurial challenges. In addition, the external informal relationship has also appeared to be an important determinant in managing women enterprises as such relationships provide emotional support and streamline the entrepreneurial work process. Therefore, the creation of social relationships is considered as an important skill for women entrepreneurs to operate within the family business challenges and avoid overlap between the home and business spheres (Ayatakshi-Endow and Steele, 2021). In Brazil, women account for a portion of business ventures relatively similar to men. However, the rate of success of women entrepreneurs is relatively lower in the context of owning and operating new enterprises. Despite a strong female entrepreneurial motivation in Brazil, fewer women continue as entrepreneurs over a long time due to imbalances in family and business commitments. The social media has increased the interpersonal interactions, which helps in reaching out to crowd information and collective intelligence to support the remote operations of the women entrepreneurs. Some women enterprises, which have technologically advanced and are founded on digital networks, have redefined their business model based on technologically and sustainably manufacturing products, and reducing waste. Such products are notable in locally manufactured women's wear made of Brazilian patented fabrics, which can be considered as good examples of women enterprises. The products manufactured in women's enterprises have also achieved notable market share in periodical markets (street markets) and have grown as unbranded entrepreneurial products led by women.

There is about 50% of women-owned small and medium enterprises, which face the financial gap in operating and growing their business. Despite gender equality being central to the development agenda in

Brazil, the women entrepreneurs' access to institutional finance remains questionable. Facing this challenge, women entrepreneurs have been observed taking an approach different than men to thinking and acting in exploring low-resource enterprises and earning desired income through marketing products and services within the niche. However, international organizations like International Bank for Reconstruction and Development are playing a catalytic role in helping local financial institutions through refinancing programs to provide financial support to women entrepreneurs for sustainable and profitable micro and small ventures.

Entrepreneurship in China

Globally, women's participation in entrepreneurship at the grassroots of society is relatively lower than men. However, in China, the women entrepreneurship is increasing, as some studies reveal that the entrepreneurial propensity among women is at par with men in terms of contributing to the regional economy, per capita income, and social values and lifestyle. Entrepreneurial growth in conventional societies depends on matrilineal and patriarchal practices, which determine the inheritance of enterprises. These practices embed both prosperity and risk perceptions while working with the ancestral enterprises. Mosuo is one of the conventional matrilineal societies which encourages women entrepreneurship as an inherited asset, and most women in this society are working with tourism enterprise. This society has a Buddhist influence wherein gender equality is one of the prime concerns. Most women in this community own or inherit property and are engaged in both farm and non-farm activities (Gong et al., 2015). Similar social practices have been found also among the Garo and Khasi community in Meghalaya state in India, which follows matrilineal social practices. The entrepreneurial activities in matrilineal communities are limited to micro- and small-scale manufacturing and services.

Most women entrepreneurs are engaged in handicrafts, textile manufacturing, pottery, and silk textile and apparels. Besides, a large number of women entrepreneurs are engaged in services within the niche such as retailing. The work-family balance is largely supported by the extended family, which enables women entrepreneurs to focus on entrepreneurial innovation and routine business management activities (Shahriar, 2018). The prospects of upward mobility of women in China has substantially supported vertical entrepreneurship by improving innovation and skills within the area of entrepreneurial specialization. Over the twentieth century, several micro institutions in China have shown evidence in promoting women entrepreneurship, which has encouraged women to engage in social enterprises, social networks, and design co-creations to promote their entrepreneurship. The upward mobility toward exploring new markets has significantly encouraged women entrepreneurs to put more efforts in driving entrepreneurial performance beyond niche markets and to overcome social limitations. Consequently, women entrepreneurs have been successful in starting businesses over the region and pushed their products through export agents. Such upward mobility has had a stronger positive effect among women to achieve economic empowerment against the conventional financial constraints (Wang et al., 2021). The upward mobility to new markets has raised higher expectations and developed risk-taking abilities in measuring the market demand and managing entrepreneurial investments (own and angel investors).

Women entrepreneurs in China have exhibited the abilities to take high risk and challenges in entrepreneurial activities. The entrepreneurial success in niche markets has led most women entrepreneurs to seek macro-institutional support for expanding entrepreneurial activities. However, in transitional economies, the quality of institutional support, resource limitations, tax liabilities, informal property rights, credit limitations, and conventional resources distribution system often narrows down the scope of entrepreneurial growth and upward mobility to new markets (Yueh, 2019). Most women entrepreneurs in China have subsistence economy, and they survive on minimum wages due to the lack of risk-taking abilities and the community push to grow beyond the bottom of the pyramid economic ecosystem. Therefore, entrepreneurial activities beyond niche discourage women entrepreneurs from exploring large-scale enterprises. The major problem with micro and small enterprises in China is the marketing of innovative products due to high transactional costs including transportation and inventory. Consequently, prospective women entrepreneurs look for institutional sponsorship to coevolve with parent institutions to enable them to approach upstream markets and develop profitable ventures (Kong et al., 2021).

The increasing financial knowledge among entrepreneurs is reducing the incidence of uncertainties in entrepreneurship, as the increase in financial knowledge helps entrepreneurs explore profitable investment, reduce costs, and increase the possibilities of incremental profitability for innovative products. Nonetheless, it has been observed that risk-neutral individuals are more likely to grow as entrepreneurs, while the risk-averse and individuals with economic uncertainty prefer to get employed in enterprises (Hu, 2014). Since the mid-twentieth century, internal migration in China has created the need to develop micro and small enterprises as a survival occupation. The migration experiences have encouraged women entrepreneurs to explore the human capital, develop innovative ideas, and strengthen their family economy by engaging in enterprises that are comparatively advantageous with their native occupations. The immigrant entrepreneurs in China have benefitted from low-cost technologies and community innovations supported by collective intelligence. Increasing internal migration combined with rapid urbanization and growing markets have promoted a rational allocation of human capital and factors of production comprising land, labor, capital, technology, and managerial know-how. Such integrated economic effect encourages entrepreneurship within the local economy, which leads to improving the household income, market attractiveness, and social values and lifestyle (Combes et al., 2017).

In the growing urbanization and expanding markets, entrepreneurs have more choices toward entrepreneurial trade from the point of view of cost structure, expected income, market demand, and perceived use value of consumers. The economically viable enterprises grow rapidly in urban areas as they meet heterogeneous consumer demand at affordable prices. In addition, the low cost of technology and frugal innovations attract urban consumers toward innovative products with utilitarian value to substitute the existing commercial products. Most Chinese enterprises develop price-based business model, which inculcates consciousness among consumers toward value for money and develop loyalty for local entrepreneurial products against the commercial brands (Zhang et al., 2021). The span of occupational varieties, the challenging experiences in urban destinations, and the availability of institutional support have shown significant effect in entrepreneurial expansion in urban China. These attributes associated with urbanization have induced ownership enterprises against seeking employment in public and corporate institutions. Consequently, family enterprises have also expanded in China using social networks and utilizing collective intelligence to develop innovative products and position them in upstream markets amidst growing consciousness of consumers toward entrepreneurial products. The experience-based entrepreneurship has significantly attracted a pool of entrepreneurs to develop a consortium entrepreneurial model, in which individual entrepreneurs work on the manufacturing of assigned products with centralized design and quality control. Such entrepreneurial guild has been experienced in the consumer electronics industry, which is contributing innovative products not only to urban destinations within China, but also in international destinations (Cheng & Smyth, 2021).

The higher entrepreneurial education has encouraged entrepreneurs in China to establish consortium entrepreneurial firms and operate effectively in larger market segments. The educated entrepreneurs work on continuous innovation in both farm and non-farm sectors and understand the changing market ecosystem to make necessary adjustments to maintain the entrepreneurial growth (Sorgner et al., 2017). Efficient allocation of entrepreneurial resources and family support in China have significantly contributed to entrepreneurial activities. The coexistence of diversified entrepreneurial activities across farm and non-farm sectors have significantly exhibited the risk substitution effect between both sectors. Consequently, the entrepreneurship in China is growing ambidextrously in both sectors with innovative product designs, diversified utilitarian perspectives, and conscious consumerism in the context of price and innovation. Entrepreneurial scope and artisanal intentions toward developing ownership and consortium enterprises is dominated by innovation-driven perspectives. Such entrepreneurial ecosystem has motivated women entrepreneurs in China to rapidly increase their performance over temporal and spatial dimensions, which has led Chinese enterprises to grow faster than the enterprises in developed countries including the United States, United Kingdom, Germany, and Japan. The social culture and entrepreneurial traditions have encouraged family enterprises to grow competitively within the regional ecosystem and optimize the allocation of resources to match with business dynamics by reducing the incidence of uncertainty (Li et al., 2021).

Global Perspectives on Women Entrepreneurs

Women entrepreneurs have attained international concern over the years, and international organizations are working in association with local governments to empower women entrepreneurs and provide gender equality for unilateral socioeconomic growth. The participation of women entrepreneurs in farm and non-farm economic activities in the developing economies has significantly increased since the mid-twentieth century despite the social and cultural stigma. Public policies in developing countries have supported women entrepreneurship through trade development skills, institutional finance, technology, and marketing of entrepreneurial products. The social governance in developing countries has encouraged women's participation in manufacturing and services enterprises that are evolved locally and have the potential for expansion beyond the niche. Although the women's participation in entrepreneurial activities has been significantly pushed by the government, social institutions, and international organizations, there exists a gender performance gap at the bottom of the pyramid. The entrepreneurial education among women has been a major concern to generate macrolevel awareness about the information on institutional finance, technology, innovation, and potential markets. These factors improve entrepreneurial performance in an integrated and coordinated manner in lieu of individual focus on each factor.

One of the major challenges in developing countries is to provide holistic support to women entrepreneurs through a single window by integrating all the above factors. In most developing economies, the public policies attend on various entrepreneurial attributes and needs by factors such as institutional finance, technology, skill development, and marketing, which have often isolated effect on performance. The social institutions play a significant role in developing women entrepreneurship and have shown success in various destinations, but replication of such models is often a difficult proposition due to sociocultural and political ideological differences. Therefore, uniform development of women entrepreneurs in developing countries appears to be a far cry. Nonetheless, some countries with outward orientation like China and India have made significant progress in promoting women enterprises and achieving significant change in socioeconomic and quality of life among women entrepreneurs. Urbanization and the tendency of upward mobility in developing countries have motivated women entrepreneurs to explore new entrepreneurial avenues with high growth potential within the growing urban and suburban neighborhood. The effective allocation of resources, access to digital networks, and motivation for self-learning among women entrepreneurs have shown encouraging results in developing economies. Consequently, women entrepreneurs have grown competitive, acquired transformational leadership, and developed capabilities to analyze the push and pull drivers to make enterprises market-oriented and generate consumer consciousness toward generic entrepreneurial products.

The earlier discussion in the chapter on women entrepreneurs in reference to five selected countries representing the developing economies scenarios is abridged in the following discussion with illustration in Fig. 6.1.

In the context of India, the major concern of public policies is to generate economic empowerment among women entrepreneurs by allocating resources required for effective functioning of an enterprise. The public policies in India provide institutional finance support and entrepreneurial training through craft development centers across destinations in the country to encourage women to build their own enterprises. The government support is evident for micro and small enterprises owned by women. The social institutions transfer knowledge, skills, and technology to women entrepreneurs to make them independent to operate their enterprises with minimum costs and high performance. In addition, collective intelligence provides substantial knowledge backup on emerging market trends, frugal innovations, corporate alliances, and managerial skills. With the advancement of information technology and contemporary business knowledge, women enterprises are also seeking crowdfunding and stakeholder investment including the resource mobilization from Angel investors.

Women entrepreneurs in Mexico evolve out of family businesses with resource limitation and conventional concepts on manufacturing and marketing. The women entrepreneurs in this region largely operate in niche market with traditional designs in textile, educational toys, food products, and fashion accessories. Most women entrepreneurs suffer from a work-life balance in Mexico due to family disruptions, which affects their entrepreneurial activity in terms of manufacturing, marketing, and income generation. Most micro and small enterprises in Mexico are engaged in manufacturing ethnic products, which have the potential to be marketed in upstream markets domestically or at international destinations. Such products include handicrafts, handlooms, and fashion accessories besides services.

In African destinations, women entrepreneurs are largely engaged in agrarian activities. Women are engaged in many small farm enterprises with financial limitations. These entrepreneurs usually lack in obtaining adequate market information to support their manufacturing activities based on market demand and consumer preferences. Women entrepreneurs in Africa are largely labor-intensive and are oriented toward generating family income rather than prospecting for commercial growth

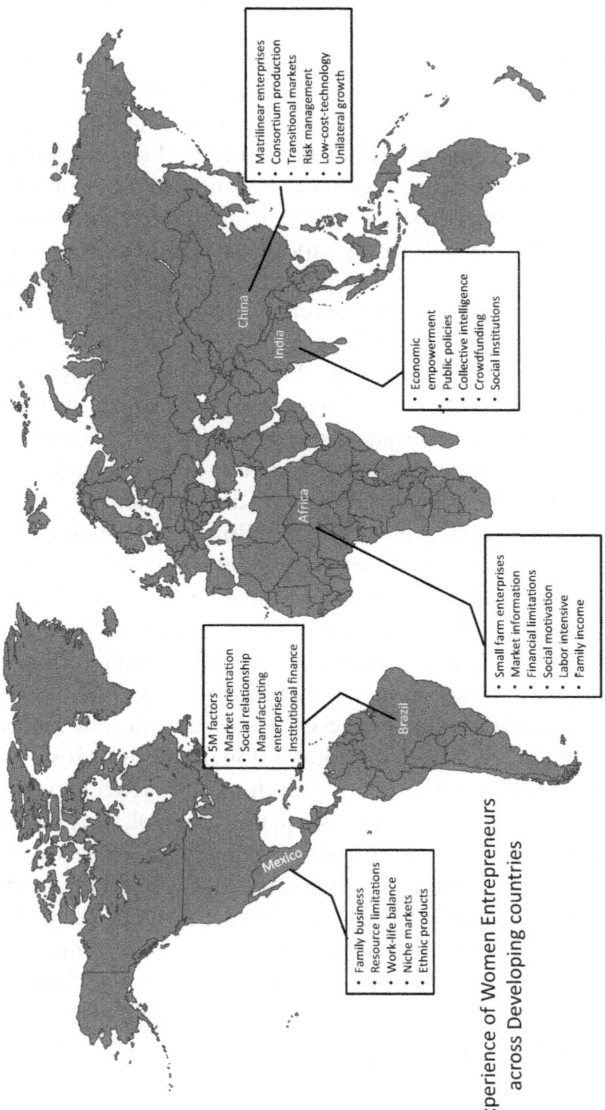

Fig. 6.1 Women entrepreneurship around the World (*Source* Author)

of their enterprises. However, social institutions are actively participating in promoting women entrepreneurs and empowering them for economic independence.

Women entrepreneurs in Brazil also evolve around family businesses and family-related economic context which helps them in managing entrepreneurial ventures and seek support for work-life balance. These entrepreneurs manage their enterprises integrating 5 M factors comprising marketing, money, management, motherhood, and intrinsic and extrinsic motivations. Women entrepreneurs in Brazil are largely successful due to the market-centric manufacturing and marketing approaches. The success factors are also supported by strong social relationships within and outside the family, which helps women entrepreneurs not only in the management of micro and small entrepreneurial ventures, but also in ensuring continuous improvement through frugal innovation and embedded services. The Brazilian enterprises have weak institutional finance resources; however, international institutions have penetrated the Brazilian economy to support the farm and non-farm enterprises at the bottom of the pyramid for regional economic development.

Chinese society has several conventional philosophies which have been transformed into entrepreneurial activities over time. The matrilinear enterprises significantly empower women entrepreneurs in owning and managing micro and small enterprises. These enterprises have evolved over time with the dynamics of market and learned manufacturing trends according to the changing consumer preferences. Consequently, women enterprises in China have reasonable access to markets despite transitions in the market, which are based on international trends. Most women enterprises in China follow a consortium production practice in which the product design, manufacturing process, quality control, and marketing strategies are centralized with the owner entrepreneurs while the manufacturing of producers is assigned to individual entrepreneurs or artisans. The consortium production is popular in the consumer electronics and fashion accessories segments. This approach helps in managing the costs and technology toward low-end manufacturing and embedding acceptable value with the products by reducing the probability of risk. Such entrepreneurial practices help women entrepreneurs to grow unilaterally within the country.

In view of the development of women entrepreneurs across developing economies, besides various socioeconomic and technology factors, the individualistic perspective of entrepreneurial growth also contributes significantly. It has been observed that most women enterprises outgrow the family businesses and have specific interest in entrepreneurial growth and governance, which requires liberal values and thinking among women entrepreneurs. As these enterprises evolve with limited resources, they often fail in addressing the social issues and problems and succumb to the entrepreneurial zeal, innovative ideas, entrepreneurial ideas, and commercialization prospects (Borzaga & Bodini, 2014). Therefore, most women enterprises depend on the social (fraternity) and family support to construct their commercial ideas and grow their entrepreneurial business. In addition, access to social services such as health, culture, leisure, and welfare provide a major contribution to grow as a stand-alone entrepreneur amidst the social complexities and individual ambitions. Making an entrepreneurial space through social conventions and market competition, most women entrepreneurs get entangled within the attributes of LIFE framework and face challenges in carrying out the entrepreneurial vision. Consequently, the LIFE paradigm comprising Liberty, Intelligence, Fraternity, and Equity makes significant contributions in initiating, structuring, managing, and leading the women enterprises among the growing market competition.

References

Ackah, C. (2013). Non-farm employment and income in rural Ghana. *Journal of International Development, 25*(3), 325–339.

Ayatakshi-Endow, S., & Steele, J. (2021). Striving for balance: Women entrepreneurs in Brazil, their multiple gendered roles and Covid-19. *International Journal of Gender and Entrepreneurship, 13*(2), 121–141.

Besbes, O., Fraiman, N. M., Olivares, M., Quinteros, M. J., & Weintraub, G. Y. (2012). *Beleza Natural*. Columbia Business School.

Borzaga, C., & Bodini, R. (2014). What to make of social innovation? Towards a framework for policy development. *Social Policy Society, 13*(3), 411–421.

Brambila, C. G., Kalis, V., Valencia-Herrera, H., Zelaya, E., & Herrera, P. G. (2013). Jugaré: Education Toys from Mexico. In M. F. Guillen (Ed). *Women entrepreneurs: Inspiring stories from emerging economies and developing countries*. Taylor & Francis.

Cheng, Z., & Smyth, R. (2021). Education and migrant entrepreneurship in urban China. *Journal of Economic Behavior & Organization, 188* (C), 506–529. https://doi.org/10.1016/j.jebo.2021.05.040

Combes, P. P., Démurger, S., & Li, S. (2017). Productivity gains from agglomeration and migration in the People's Republic of China between 2002 and 2013. *Asian Development Review, 34*(2), 184–200.

Dieterich, C., Hakura, C., & Newiak, M. (2016). In the Driver's seat. *Finance & Development, 53*(2), 22–24.

Gong, B., Yan, H., & Yang, C. L. (2015). Gender differences in the dictator experiment: Evidence from the matrilineal Mosuo and the patriarchal Yi. *Experimental Economics, 18*(2), 302–313.

Henry, C., Foss, L., & Ahl, H. (2016). Gender and entrepreneurship research: A review of methodological approaches. *International Small Business Journal, 34*(3), 217–241.

Hu, F. (2014). Risk attitudes and self-employment in China. *China & World Economy, 22*(3), 101–120.

Li, R., Wang, T., & Zhou, M. (2021). Entrepreneurship and household portfolio choice: Evidence from the China household finance survey. *Journal of Empirical Finance, 60*(1), 1–15.

Kaciak, E., & Welsh, D. H. B. (2020). Women entrepreneurs and work–life interface: The impact of sustainable economies on success. *Journal of Business Research, 112*(15), 281–290.

Khaire, M., & McGinn, K. L. (2010). *SEWA Trade Facilitation Center: Changing the Spool*. Harvard Business Scholl Press.

Kong, D., Qin, N., & Xiang, J. (2021, September). Minimum wage and entrepreneurship: Evidence from China. *Journal of Economic Behavior & Organization, 189*, 320–336.

Lecuna, A., Cohen, B., & Chavez, R. (2017). Characteristics of high-growth entrepreneurs in Latin America. *International Entrepreneurship and Management Journal, 13*(1), 141–159.

Nagler, P., & Naudé, W. (2017). Non-farm entrepreneurship in rural sub-Saharan Africa: New empirical evidence. *Food Policy, 67*, 175–191.

Ojong, N., Simba, A., & Dana, L. H. (2021). Female entrepreneurship in Africa: A review, trends, and future research directions. *Journal of Business Research, 132*(2), 233–248.

Patnaik, A. (2021, October 6). Women entrepreneurship: The weak link in India's growth story. *The Times of India*.

Premchander, S. (2003). NGOs and local MFIs—How to increase poverty reduction through women's small and micro-enterprise. *Futures, 35*(4), 361–378.

Rajagopal, R. S., Burgos, F., & Gamboa, L. (2013). The spirit behind Talavera de la Reyna: Angelca Moreno's Pottery, In M. F. Guillen (Ed.), *Women entrepreneurs: Inspiring stories from emerging economies and developing countries*. Routledge.

Shahriar, A. Z. M. (2018). Gender differences in entrepreneurial propensity: Evidence from matrilineal and patriarchal societies. *Journal of Business Venturing, 33*(6), 762–779.

Sorgner, A., Fritsch, M., & Kritikos, A. (2017). Do entrepreneurs really earn less? *Small Business Economics, 49*(2), 251–272.

van Rooyen, C., Stewart, R., & de Wet, T. (2012). The impact of microfinance in Sub-Saharan Africa: A systematic review of the evidence. *World Development, 40*(11), 2249–2262.

Wale, E., Chipfupa, U., & Hadebe, N. (2021). *Towards identifying enablers and inhibitors to on-farm entrepreneurship: Evidence from smallholders in KwaZulu-Natal, South Africa, Heliyon, 7*(1), https://doi.org/10.1016/j.heliyon.2020.e05660

Wang, L., Liu, L., & Dai, Y. (2021). Owning your future: Entrepreneurship and the prospects of upward mobility in China. *Economic Modelling*. https://doi.org/10.1016/j.econmod.2021.105637

Yueh, L. (2019). Self-employment in urban China: Networking in a transition economy. *China Economic Review, 20*(3), 471–484.

Zhang, S., Qiu, L., & Zhao, D. (2021). Technological diffusion, migration and entrepreneurship in China. *Journal of Asian Economics*. https://doi.org/10.1016/j.asieco.2021.101322

Index

A. Rajagopal, *Women Entrepreneurs in Emerging Markets*, International Marketing and Management Research,
https://doi.org/10.1007/978-3-030-89770-3

R

S

T

U

V

W

The manufacturer's authorised representative in the EU is Springer Nature Customer Service Centre GmbH, Europaplatz 3, 69115 Heidelberg, Germany. If you have any concerns regarding our products, please contact ProductSafety@springernature.com

Printed and bound by CPI Group (UK) Ltd, Croydon, CR0 4YY
30/09/2026
02225475-0016